Divorce
in Florida

The Legal Process,
Your Rights, and What to Expect

Lisa P. Kirby, Esq.
Shayna K. Cavanaugh, Esq.

Addicus Books
Omaha, Nebraska

An Addicus Nonfiction Book

ISBN 978-1-940495-98-9

Typography by Jack Kusler

This book is not intended to serve as a substitute for an attorney. Nor is it the author's intent to give legal advice contrary to that of an attorney.

Library of Congress Cataloging-in-Publication Data

Names: Kirby, Lisa P., — author. | Cavanaugh, Shayna K., — author.
Title: Divorce in Florida : the legal process, your rights, and what to expect / Lisa P. Kirby, Esq., Shayna K. Cavanaugh, Esq.
Description: Omaha, Nebraska : Addicus Books, Inc., 2016. | Includes index. | "An Addicus nonfiction book."
Identifiers: LCCN 2016025234 (print) | LCCN 2016025640 (e-book) | ISBN 9781940495989 (alk. paper) | ISBN 9781943886524 (PDF) | ISBN 9781943886548 (MOBI) | ISBN 9781943886531 (EPUB)
Subjects: LCSH: Divorce—Law and legislation—Florida—Miscellanea.
Classification: LCC KFF100 .K57 2016 (print) | LCC KFF100 (e-book) | DDC
346.75901/66—dc23
LC record available at https://lccn.loc.gov/2016025234

Addicus Books, Inc.
P.O. Box 45327
Omaha, Nebraska 68145
www.AddicusBooks.com
Printed in the United States of America
10 9 8 7 6 5 4 3 2 1

Contents

Acknowledgments

We extend a special thank you to all our clients who both shared their stories with us and placed their trust in us as we helped them through difficult times in their lives.

We also thank our families for their support while we were writing this book. Also, we express our appreciation to Rod Colvin and Jack Kusler, of Addicus Books, who encouraged us to write this book.

Introduction

Nearly every day we meet with people who are struggling as they move through a divorce. Whether you are initiating the divorce or responding to the divorce, you are facing a change in every single part of your life. No aspect of your life remains untouched from the divorce process. Whether it is parenting, family relationships, finances, social networks, personal belongings, a residence, job performance —your entire personal world is impacted by a divorce. Our purpose in writing this book was educate you and to help guide you through this uncertain journey.

No matter what, divorce can be difficult. We work with courageous clients, like you, to help them make tough decisions in the face of their changing life. We know from our experience in working with hundreds of clients over the years, that in order to reach a place of growth and healing, you will need a tremendous amount of support as you work through the process.

We wrote *Divorce in Florida* to help you move through this life transition with more clarity and ease. It is not intended to be a substitute for advice from a lawyer. It is merely designed to assist you in partnering with your lawyer to reach your goals in the resolution of your divorce.

In writing *Divorce in Florida,* we have endeavored to give you guidance and explain the steps in the process in hopes that it will empower you. The more understanding, control, and clarity you have throughout the process, the better you are able to make sound decisions. We hope that the information will help you see the big picture of the emotional journey you're currently taking.

During your divorce, you will have hard, grief-filled days and you will face many uncertainties, but you will get through them. In the end, you will find relief in the letting go of old sadness. You'll see glimmers of hope as you recreate yourself, and you'll see new possibilities for the future.

Lisa P. Kirby, Esq.
Shayna K. Cavanaugh, Esq.

1

Understanding the Divorce Process

At a time when you feel that your life is in utter chaos, sometimes the smallest bit of predictability can bring a sense of comfort. The outcome of many aspects of your divorce are unpredictable, driving up your fear and anxiety. But there is one part of your divorce that does have some measure of certainty, and that is the divorce process itself.

Most divorces proceed in a step-by-step manner. Despite the uniqueness of your divorce, you can generally count on one phase of your divorce following the next. Sometimes just realizing you are completing stages and moving forward with your divorce can reassure you that it will eventually come to an end.

Having an understanding of the divorce process can lower your anxiety when your attorney starts talking about "discovery," "depositions," "mediation," or "going to trial" and you feel your heart start pounding in fear. It can reduce your frustration about the length of the process because you understand why each step is needed. Your knowledge will support you as you begin to prepare for each step along the way.

Most importantly, understanding the divorce process will make your experience of the entire divorce easier. Who wouldn't prefer that?

1.1   Do I have to hire an attorney to get a divorce in Florida?

You are not required to have an attorney to obtain a divorce in Florida. However, if your case involves children, alimony, significant property, or debts, you should at least con-

1

sult with an attorney before deciding whether to proceed on your own. You may have certain rights and obligations about which you are unaware.

If your divorce doesn't involve any of these issues, it is still advisable to consult with an attorney to discuss the best way to proceed. A person who proceeds in a legal matter without a lawyer is referred to as being *pro se* (pronounced pro-say), on one's own. Most of the forms you will need to be able to proceed *pro se* are available online at www.flcourts.org at no cost to you.

1.2   What is the first step?

If you decide to consult with an attorney, find a law firm that handles divorces as a regular part of their law practice. The best recommendations come from people who have knowledge of a lawyer's experience and reputation. If you do not feel comfortable asking someone you know, you can call either your local bar association or the Florida Bar Association for a local referral.

Even if you are not ready to file for divorce, but think your spouse may be, call to schedule an appointment right away to obtain information about protecting yourself and your children. The more information you have the better you are prepared if your spouse does files for divorce.

When you contact the attorney for your consultation, ask what documents you should bring to the initial meeting. Try to make a list of your questions to bring to your first meeting. Make sure you are aware of whether and how much the attorney charges for a consultation.

1.3   Is Florida a no-fault state or do I need grounds for a divorce?

Florida, like most states, is a no-fault divorce state. This means that neither you nor your spouse is required to prove that the other is "at fault" in order to be granted a divorce. Factors such as infidelity, domestic violence, or abandonment are not necessary to receive a divorce in Florida. Rather, it is only necessary to prove that the marriage is "irretrievably broken" to have it dissolved.

2

The testimony of either you or your spouse that the marriage is "irretrievably broken" is sufficient evidence for the court to rule that the marriage should be dissolved. The judge will not ask for information regarding the nature of the problems that led to the divorce or whether any type of reconciliation efforts were made.

1.4 Do I have to get divorced in the same state or country where I got married?

No. Regardless of where you were married, you may seek a divorce in Florida if the jurisdictional requirements of residency are met and the marriage was a legal marriage in the state or country where you were married.

1.5 How long do I have to have lived in Florida to get a divorce in the state?

Either you or your spouse must have been a resident of Florida for at least six months prior to filing the divorce to meet the residency requirement for a divorce in Florida. If neither party meets the residency requirement, other legal options may be available for your protection. If you do not meet the six-month residency requirement, talk to your attorney about these other options.

1.6 My spouse has told me he or she will never "give me" a divorce. Can I get one in Florida anyway?

Yes. Florida does not require that your spouse "agree to" a divorce. If your spouse threatens to "not give you a divorce," know that in Florida this is an idle threat without any basis in the law.

Under Florida law, to obtain a divorce you will only need to testify that your marriage is "irretrievably broken." Evidence of this will be your testimony at a final hearing. It is not necessary to have your spouse agree to the divorce or to allege the specific details that caused the filing of a divorce to obtain a divorce in Florida.

The Divorce Process

To initiate the divorce process, in Florida the following are typically the first steps:

- Obtain a referral for an attorney.
- Schedule an appointment with the attorney.
- Prepare questions and gather necessary documents for an initial consultation.
- Meet for an initial consultation with an attorney.
- Sign a retainer agreement and pay a *retainer fee* (an initial fee to the attorney to begin your divorce process) to the attorney.
- Provide requested information and documents to your attorney.
- Attorney prepares the *summons and petition for dissolution* for your review and signature.
- Attorney files the summons and petition with the clerk of the court.
- The clerk will issue the summons and, in some counties, a standing order. A *standing order* explains your rights and responsibilities while the divorce is pending in the courts.
- Process server serves the summons, petition, and standing order on the respondent.

If you have been served with divorce papers:

- Obtain a referral for an attorney.
- Schedule an appointment with the attorney.
- Prepare questions and gather necessary documents for an initial consultation.
- Meet for an initial consultation with an attorney.
- Sign a retainer agreement and pay a retainer fee to the attorney.
- Provide requested information and documents to your attorney.
- Attorney prepares an *answer* and, if necessary, a *counter-petition* for your review and signature.

- Attorney files your answer with the clerk of the court within twenty days of service of the summons and petition on you.

After an action has been commenced and the answer filed:

- Complete your financial affidavit and gather supporting documents (mandatory disclosure).
- Negotiations begin regarding a temporary parenting schedule, child and spousal support, payment of marital obligations, and attorney fees.
- Attorney prepares motions for any requests for temporary relief not previously made.
- If there are minor children, the parties comply with any local rules or court orders to attend a parent education course.
- Court holds hearing(s) on requests for temporary relief.
- Either the parties reach an agreement or the court issues temporary orders.
- Temporary order is prepared by one attorney, approved as to form by other attorney, and submitted to the judge for signature.
- Both sides conduct *discovery*—the process designed to obtain information regarding all relevant facts, and commence the process to exchange valuations of all assets, including expert opinions if needed.
- You confer with your attorney to review facts, identify issues, assess strengths and weaknesses of case, review strategy, and possibly develop a settlement proposal.
- Spouses, with the support of their attorneys, attempt to reach agreement through written proposals, settlement conferences, or other forms of negotiation.

If you reach an agreement on all issues, then:

- One attorney prepares the marital settlement agreement and necessary final judgment paperwork.
- Both parties and their attorneys sign agreement and all necessary paperwork.
- Final judgment paperwork is filed with the court.

- The court holds a brief final hearing.
- Final judgment is entered and you will be divorced.

If you are unable to reach an agreement on all issues, then:

- Parties attend mandatory mediation.
- Your attorney completes all necessary discovery to get you and your case ready for trial.
- Your attorney files a *notice for trial.*
- If an agreement has been reached on any issues, your attorney prepares a stipulation on those issues. All other issues are set for trial.
- You work with your attorney to prepare your case for trial.
- Your attorney prepares witnesses, trial exhibits, legal research on contested issues, pretrial motions, trial briefs, direct and cross-examination of witnesses, opening statements, witness subpoenas, and your closing argument.
- You meet with your attorney for final trial preparation.
- Trial is held.
- The judge will either give an oral ruling and have one of the attorneys prepare a proposed final judgment or the judge will prepare the final judgment.
- Once the judge signs the final judgment you will be divorced.

Your post-trial rights are discussed in the section on appeals.

1.7   Can I divorce my spouse in Florida if he or she lives in another state?

Provided you have met the residency requirements of living in Florida for six months, you can file for divorce here even if your spouse lives in another state. It is important, however, that although you may be able to get divorced, other rights you may have as a result of the divorce may not be available to you.

Discuss with your attorney the facts that will need to be proven and the steps necessary to give your spouse proper notice to ensure that the court will have jurisdiction over your spouse. Your attorney can counsel you on whether it is possible to proceed with the divorce.

1.8 How can I divorce my spouse when I don't know where this person lives now?

Florida law allows you to proceed with a divorce even if you do not know the current address of your spouse.

First, take action to attempt to locate your spouse. Contact family members, friends, former coworkers, or anyone else who might know your spouse's whereabouts. Use resources on the internet that are designed to help locate people.

Let your attorney know the efforts you have made to attempt to find your spouse. Inform your lawyer of your spouse's last known address, as well as any work address or other address where this person may be found. Once your attorney attempts to serve your spouse without success, it is possible to ask the court to proceed with the divorce by giving notice through publication in a newspaper.

While your divorce may be granted following service of notice by publication in a newspaper, you may not be able to get other court orders such as those for child support or alimony without giving personal notice to your spouse. Talk to your attorney about your options and rights if you don't know where your spouse is living.

1.9 I just moved to a different county. Do I have to file in the county where my spouse lives?

You need to file for divorce in the county where you and your spouse last resided as husband and wife.

1.10 I immigrated to Florida. Will my immigration status stop me from getting a divorce?

If you meet the six-month residency requirement for a divorce in Florida, you can get a divorce regardless of your immigration status. Talk to your immigration lawyer about the likelihood of a divorce leading to immigration challenges.

If you are a victim of domestic violence, tell your lawyer. You may be eligible for a change in your immigration status under the federal *Violence Against Women Act*.

1.11   Is there a waiting period for a divorce in Florida?

Yes. Florida judges must wait twenty-one days from the date the divorce is filed to enter a final judgment.

1.12   What is a *divorce petition*?

A *divorce petition*, also referred to as a *petition for dissolution of marriage* is a document signed by the person filing for divorce and filed with the clerk of the court to initiate the divorce process. The petition will set forth in very general terms what the petitioner is asking the court to order.

1.13   My spouse said she filed for divorce last week, but my lawyer says there is nothing on file at the courthouse. What does it mean to "file for divorce?"

When attorneys use the term "filing" they are ordinarily referring to filing a legal document. All documents in Florida are required to be filed electronically through an e-filing portal. Once the documents are submitted electronically, they are considered "filed" when the clerk has accepted them for filing. This process normally takes one to two days.

1.14   If we both want a divorce, does in matter who files?

For purposes of the court, the court does not give an advantage to either the *petitioner,* the filing party, or the *respondent,* the non-filing party.

Your attorney may advise you to file first or to wait for your spouse to file, depending upon the overall strategy for your case and your circumstances. For example, if there is a concern that your spouse will either transfer assets or incur debts upon learning about your plans for divorce, your attorney might advise you to file first. However, if you are separated from your spouse but have a beneficial temporary arrangement, your attorney may counsel you to wait for your spouse to file.

You and your attorney should work together to make the decision about whether and when to initiate the legal process by filing a petition for dissolution of marriage.

1.15   Is my divorce published in the newspaper?

No, Florida does not publish divorce information in the newspaper unless you have to publish the petition for divorce for service of process. However, almost all divorce records are public records.

1.16   Is there a way to avoid embarrassing my spouse and not have the sheriff serve him with the divorce papers at his workplace?

Your spouse can be served at whatever address you provide to your attorney. Servicing your spouse at work is not necessary if you can provide a alternate location where your spouse can be served.

1.17   Should I sign an *acceptance of service* even if I don't agree with what my spouse has written in the complaint for divorce?

Signing the *acceptance of service* does not mean that you agree with anything your spouse has stated in the divorce petition or anything that your spouse is asking for in the divorce.

Signing the acceptance of service only substitutes for having the sheriff personally hand you the documents. You do not waive the right to object to anything your spouse has stated in the complaint for dissolution of marriage. Once you sign the acceptance of service, you need to answer the petition within twenty days.

Follow your attorney's advice on whether and when to sign an acceptance of service.

1.18   Why should I contact an attorney right away if I have received divorce papers?

If you are either served with divorce papers or have received divorce papers from your spouse, it is important that you obtain legal advice as soon as possible. It is important to contact an attorney immediately because in Florida you only have twenty days to respond to the papers. If you do not file a response within the twenty days, default could be entered against you. If a default is entered against you, you could be prohibited from being able to present your side of the case to the court or receiving any further notice from your spouse or the court that the matter is going forward.

1.19 What is an *ex parte* court order?

An *ex parte* court order is obtained by one party going to the judge to ask for something without giving prior notice or an opportunity to be heard by the other side.

With the exception of restraining orders, judges are reluctant to sign *ex parte* orders. Ordinarily the court will require the other side to have notice of any requests for court orders, and a hearing before the judge will be held.

An *affidavit,* which is a written statement sworn under oath, is usually required before a judge will sign an *ex parte* order. *Ex parte* orders are generally limited to emergency situations such as requests for temporary restraining orders or other order to protect the safety of you or your children.

When an *ex parte* order is granted, the party who did not request the order will have an opportunity to have a subsequent hearing before the judge to determine whether the order should remain in effect.

1.20 What is a *motion?*

A *motion* is a request that the judge enter a court order of some type. For example, your attorney may file a written motion with the court asking for a temporary parenting plan and child support.

Some motions are made to handle certain procedural aspects of your case, such as a motion for a continuance asking that a court date be changed or a motion for extension of time asking that the court extend a deadline. In some cases, a motion may be made orally rather than in writing, such as when an issue arises during the course of a court hearing or trial.

1.21 Once my petition for divorce is filed, how long will it take before a temporary hearing is held to decide what happens with our child and our finances while the divorce is pending?

Once your spouse has received the divorce papers, you and your attorney can discuss whether it is necessary to seek temporary relief. *Temporary relief* can include, parenting issues, child support, payment of marital obligations, and spousal support. If it is necessary to request temporary relief, a hearing will be scheduled and the judge can enter a temporary relief order that addresses these issues. The temporary relief order applies while the divorce is pending.

1.22 How much notice will I get if my spouse seeks a temporary order?

Florida law requires that you receive "reasonable notice" of any court hearings. In the case of motions for temporary orders, the generally accepted amount of time is ten days notice.

1.23 During my divorce, what am I responsible for doing?

Your attorney will explain what actions you should take to further the divorce process and to help you reach the best possible outcome.

You will be asked to:

- Keep in regular contact with your attorney.
- Update your attorney regarding any changes in your contact information, such as address, phone numbers, e-mail address, and employment.
- If you have children, take the required parent education course.
- Provide your attorney with all requested documents, including financial affidavit and mandatory disclosure.
- Provide requested information in a timely manner.
- Complete forms and questionnaires.
- Appear in court on time.
- Be direct about asking any questions you might have.
- Tell your attorney your thoughts on settlement or what you would like the judge to order in your case.
- Remain respectful toward your spouse throughout the process.
- Comply with any temporary court orders, such as restraining or support orders.
- Advise your attorney of any significant developments in your case.

By doing your part in the divorce process, you enable your attorney to partner with you for a better outcome while also lowering your attorney fees.

1.24   I'm worried that I won't remember to ask my lawyer about all of the issues in my case. How can I be sure I don't miss anything?

Write down all of the topics you want to discuss with your attorney, including what your goals are for the outcome of the divorce. The better you communicate with your attorney, the easier it will be for your attorney to support you to get what you want. Realize that your attorney will think of some issues that you may not be thinking of. Your lawyer's experience will be helpful in making sure nothing important is forgotten.

1.25   My spouse has all of our financial information. How will I be able to prepare for negotiations and trial if I don't know the facts or have the documents?

Once your divorce has been filed with the court, both parties are required to complete financial affidavits and provide mandatory disclosure. *Mandatory disclosure* includes: tax returns, bank statements, evidence of marital debts, documents evidencing the value of assets, proof of income, and proof and values of real and personal property.

If, after disclosure of the required documents, your spouse still has not provided sufficient documents, your attorney can prepare a request for your spouse to produce additional documents or subpoena the documents that have not been provided. Additional options for obtaining information (discovery) will be discussed in chapter 5.

1.26   My spouse and I both want our divorce to be amicable. How can we keep it that way?

You and your spouse are to be acknowledged for your willingness to cooperate while focusing on moving through the divorce process. This will not only make your lives easier and save you money on attorney fees, but it is also more likely to result in an outcome you are both satisfied with.

Find a lawyer who understands your goal to reach settlement and encourage your spouse to do the same. Cooperate with the prompt exchange of necessary information. If you are not able to settle all of the issues in your divorce, you can agree to participate in mediation to resolve the outstanding issues.

1.27   Can I get a different judge?

Talk to your attorney about the reasons you want a different judge. If you believe that your judge has a conflict of interest, such as having a personal relationship with any of the parties, you may have a basis for asking the judge to be removed in order to allow another judge to hear the case.

1.28   How long will it take to get my divorce?

The more you and your spouse are in agreement, the faster your divorce will conclude. If all issues, such as parenting plans/time-sharing, support, property, and debts, are completely settled between you and your spouse, a final hearing can be held after the twenty-one-day waiting period.

If your case proceeds to trial, the process can take up to a year or longer for your divorce to be final. This is discussed in more detail later in the book.

1.29   What is the significance of my divorce being final?

The divorce decree which is called a final judgment of dissolution of marriage is important for many reasons. It can affect your right to remarry, your eligibility for health insurance from your former spouse, and your filing status for income taxes.

1.30   When does my divorce become final?

In Florida, the day the judge signs your final judgment of dissolution, the official title of your divorce papers, you are considered divorced. There is no waiting period after the judge signs the paperwork that is required before you can consider yourself divorced.

1.31   Can I start using my former name right away and how do I get my name legally restored?

You may begin using your former name at any time, provided you are not doing so for any unlawful purpose, such as to avoid your creditors. Many agencies and institutions, however, will not alter their records without a court order changing your name.

If you want your former name restored, let your attorney know so that this provision can be included in your divorce decree. If you want to change your legal name after the divorce and have not provided for it in your decree, it will be necessary for you to undergo a separate legal action for a name change.

2

Coping with Stress
during the Divorce Process

No matter how long or short you have been married, you probably did not expect to be going through or considering a divorce. Like most people, you imagined your marriage to last forever when you said "I do". But, life happens, people change, or for other reasons your marriage is not what you expected.

Whatever the circumstances, the emotions and stresses of a divorce can range from one extreme to another as you go through the process. You may feel relief and ready to move on with your life. On other hand, you may feel emotions that are quite painful—anger—fear—sorrow. You could be feeling a deep sense of loss and resentment. It is important to find support for yourself to deal with all of these emotions.

Having a clear understanding of the divorce process can help to reduce the stress and emotions that you are feeling. The more understanding that you have of the divorce process, the better you will be able to make thoughtful decisions rather than on pure emotion. As you go through the divorce process ask yourself if the decisions you are making are best for you and your future or are you making them because of the emotions you are feeling. Set goals and expectations and let those guide you through the process.

2.1   My spouse left home weeks ago. I don't want a divorce because I feel our marriage can be saved. Should I still see an attorney?

It's a good idea to see an attorney. Whether you want a divorce or not, there may be important actions for you to take now to protect your assets, credit, home, children, and future right to support.

If your spouse files for divorce, you will be served and have to respond within twenty days. It is best to be prepared with the support of an attorney, even if you decide not to file for a divorce at this time.

2.2   The thought of going to a lawyer's office to talk about divorce is more than I can bear. I canceled the first appointment I made because I just couldn't do it. What should I do?

Many people going through a divorce are dealing with lawyers for the first time and feel anxious about the experience. Ask a trusted friend or family member to go with you. He or she can support you by writing down your questions in advance, by taking notes for you during the meeting, and helping you to remember what the lawyer said after the meeting is concluded. It is very likely that you will feel greatly relieved just to be better informed.

2.3   There is some information about my marriage that I think my attorney needs, but I'm too embarrassed to discuss it. Must I tell the attorney?

Your attorney has an ethical duty to maintain confidentiality. Past events in your marriage are matters that your lawyer is obligated to keep private.

Attorneys who practice divorce law are accustomed to hearing a lot of intimate information about families. While it is deeply personal to you, it is unlikely that anything you tell your lawyer will be a shock. Remember, it would be worse for your attorney to find out from your spouse's attorney or in court than you being honest and open with attorney from the beginning.

While it may feel uncomfortable for a short moment, it is important that your attorney have complete information so that your interests can be fully protected. If speaking directly about these facts still seems too hard, consider putting them in a letter.

2.4 I'm unsure about how to tell our children about the divorce, and I'm worried I'll say the wrong thing. What's the best way?

How you talk to your children about the divorce will depend upon their ages and development. Changes in your children's everyday lives, such as a change of residence or one parent leaving the home, are far more important to them. Information about legal proceedings and meetings with lawyers are best kept among adults.

Simpler answers are best for young children. Avoid giving them more information than they need. Use the adults in your life as a source of support to meet your own emotional needs.

After the initial discussion, keep the door open to further talks by creating opportunities for them to talk about the divorce. Use these times to acknowledge their feelings and offer support. Always assure them that the divorce is not their fault and that they are still loved by both you and your spouse, regardless of the divorce.

2.5 My youngest child seems very depressed about the divorce, the middle one is angry, and my teenager is skipping school. How can I cope?

A child's reaction to divorce can vary depending upon his or her age and other factors. Some may cry and beg for a reconciliation, and others may act out. Reducing conflict with your spouse, being a consistent and nurturing parent, and making sure both of you remain involved are all actions that can support your children regardless of how they are reacting to the divorce.

Support groups for children whose parents are divorcing are also available at many schools and religious communities. A school counselor can also provide support. If more help is needed, confer with a therapist experienced in working with children.

2.6   I am so frustrated by my spouse's "Disneyland" parent behavior. Is there anything I can do to stop this?

Feelings of guilt, competition, or remorse sometimes lead a parent to be tempted to spend parenting time in trips to the toy store and special activities. Other times they can result in an absence of discipline in an effort to become the favored parent or to make the time "special."

Shift your focus from the other parent's to your own, and do your best to be an outstanding parent during this time. This includes keeping a routine for your child for family meals, bedtimes, chores, and homework. Encourage family activities, as well as individual time with each child when it's possible.

During a time when child's life is changing, providing a consistent and stable routine in your home can ease their anxiety and provide comfort.

2.7   Between requests for information from my spouse's lawyer and my own lawyer, I am totally overwhelmed. How do I manage gathering all of this detailed information by the deadlines imposed?

First, simply get started. Often the thought about a task is worse than the job itself.

Second, break it down into smaller tasks. Perhaps one evening you gather your tax returns and on the weekend you work on your monthly living expenses.

Third, let in support. Ask that friend of yours who just loves numbers to come over for an evening with her calculator to help you get organized.

Finally, communicate with your lawyer. Your attorney or paralegal may be able to make your job easier by giving you suggestions or help. It may be that essential information can be provided now and the details submitted later.

2.8   I am so depressed about my divorce that I'm having difficulty getting out of bed in the morning to care for my children. What should I do?

See your health care provider. Feelings of depression are common during a divorce. You also want to make sure that you identify any physical health concerns.

Although feelings of sadness are common during a divorce, more serious depression means it's time to allow some professional support.

Your health and your ability to care for your children are both essential. Follow through on recommendations by your health care professionals for therapy, medication, or other measures to improve your wellness.

2.9   I know I need help to cope with the stress of the divorce, but I can't afford counseling. What can I do?

You are wise to recognize that divorce is a time for letting in support. You can explore a number of options, including:

- Meeting with a member of the clergy or lay chaplain
- Joining a divorce support group
- Turning to friends and family members
- Going to a therapist or divorce counselor. If budget is a concern, contact a social agency that offers counseling services on a sliding-fee scale.

If none of these options are available, look again at your budget. You may see that counseling is important enough that you decide to find a way to increase your income or lower your expenses to support this investment in your well-being.

2.10   I'm the one who filed for divorce, but I still have loving feelings toward my spouse and feel sad about divorcing. Does this mean I should dismiss my divorce?

Strong feelings of caring about your spouse often persist after a divorce is filed. Whether or not to proceed with a divorce is a deeply personal decision. While feelings can inform us of our thoughts, sometimes they can also cause us to not look at everything there is to see in our situation.

Have you and your spouse participated in marriage counseling? Has your spouse refused to seek treatment for an addiction? Are you worried about the safety of you or your children if you remain in the marriage? Can you envision yourself as financially secure if you remain in this marriage? Is your spouse involved in another relationship?

The answer to these questions can help you clarify whether to consider reconciliation. Talk to your therapist, coach, or spiritual advisor to help determine the right path for you.

2.11 Will my lawyer charge me for the time I spend talking about my feelings about my spouse and my divorce?

It depends. If you are paying your attorney by the hour, expect to be charged for the time your attorney spends talking with you. If your attorney is being paid a flat rate for handling your divorce, the time spend talking with you will be included in the fee.

2.12 My lawyer doesn't seem to realize how difficult my divorce is for me. How do I make the lawyer understand?

Everyone wants support and compassion from the professionals who are helping them during a divorce. Speak frankly with your attorney about your concerns. It may be that your lawyer does not see your concerns as being relevant to the job of getting your desired outcome in the divorce. Your willingness to improve the communication will help your lawyer understand how best to support you in the process and will help you understand which matters are best left for discussion with your therapist or a supportive friend.

2.13 I've been told not to speak ill of my spouse in front of my child, but I know my spouse is doing this all the time. Why can't I just speak the truth?

It can be devastating for your child to hear you bad-mouthing his or her other parent. What your child needs is permission to love both of you, regardless of any bad parental behavior. The best way to support your child during this time is to encourage a positive relationship with the other parent.

2.14 Nobody in our family has ever been divorced and I feel really ashamed. Will my children feel the same way?

Making a change in how you see your family identity is huge for you. The best way to help your children is to establish a sense of pride in their new family and to look forward to the future with a real sense of possibility.

Your children will have an opportunity to witness you overcoming obstacles, demonstrating independence, and moving forward in your life in spite of challenges. You can be a great teacher to them during this time by demonstrating pride in your family and in yourself.

2.15 I am terrified of having my deposition taken. My spouse's lawyer is very aggressive, and I'm afraid I'm going to say something that will hurt my case.

A deposition is an opportunity for your spouse's attorney to gather information and to assess the type of witness you will be if the case proceeds to trial. Feeling anxious about your deposition is normal. However, regardless of the personality of the lawyers, most depositions in divorces are quite uneventful.

Remember that your attorney will be seated by your side at all times to support you. Ask to meet with your lawyer in advance to prepare for the deposition. If you are worried about certain questions that might be asked, talk to your attorney about them. Think of it as an opportunity, and enlist your lawyer's support in being well prepared.

2.16 I am still so angry at my spouse. How can I be expected to sit in the same room during a mediation?

If you are still really angry at your spouse, it may be beneficial to postpone the mediation for a time. You might also consider seeking some counseling to support you with coping with your feelings of anger.

You can ask your attorney if you and your attorney can remain in one room while your spouse and his or her attorney are in another. Settlement offers are then relayed between the attorneys throughout the negotiation process. By shifting your focus from your angry feelings to your goal of a settlement, it may be easier to proceed through the process.

2.17 I'm afraid I can't make it through court without having an emotional breakdown. How do I prepare?

A divorce trial can be a highly emotional time, calling for lots of support. Some of these ideas may help you through the process:

- Meet with your lawyer or the firm's support staff in advance of your court date to prepare you for court.
- Ask your lawyer whether there are any documents you should review in preparation for court, such as your deposition.
- Visit the courtroom in advance to get comfortable with the surroundings.
- Ask your lawyer about having a support person with you on your court date.
- Ask yourself what the worst thing is that could happen and consider what options you would have if it did.
- Avoid alcohol, eat healthfully, exercise, and have plenty of rest during the period of time leading up to the court date. Each of these will help you to prepare for the emotions of the day.
- Plan what you intend to wear in advance. Small preparations will lower your stress.
- Visualize the experience going well. Picture yourself sitting in the witness chair, giving clear, confident, and truthful answers to easy questions.
- Arrive early at the courthouse and make sure you have a plan for parking your car if you are not familiar with the area.
- Take slow, deep breaths. Breathing deeply will steady your voice, calm your nerves, and improve your focus.

Your attorney will be prepared to support you throughout the proceedings. By taking the above steps, you can increase the ease of your experience.

2.18   I am really confused. One day I think I've made a mistake, the next day I know I can't go back, and a few minutes later I can hardly wait to be single again. Some days I just don't believe I'm getting divorced. What's happening?

What you are experiencing is normal for a person going through divorce. Denial, transition, and acceptance are common passages for a person going through a divorce. One moment you might feel excited about your future and a few hours later you think your life is ruined.

What can be helpful to remember is that you may not pass from one stage to the next in a direct line. Feelings of anger or sadness may well up in you long after you thought you had moved on. Similarly, your mood might feel bright one day as you think about your future plans, even though you still miss your spouse.

Taking good care of yourself is essential during this period of your life. What you are going through requires a tremendous amount of energy. Allow yourself to experience your emotions, but also continue moving forward with your life. These steps will help your life get easier day by day.

3

Working with an Attorney

If there is only one thing you can be sure of in your divorce, it's that you will be given plenty of advice. Well-intentioned friends, neighbors, cousins, and even complete strangers will be happy to tell you war stories about their ex or about their sister who got divorced in Canada or even another county or another state. Many will insist they know what you should do, even though they haven't the vaguest notion of the facts of your case or the law in Florida.

But there is one person whose advice should matter to you: your attorney. You should feel confident that your lawyer is giving you the advice that is right for you and for your situation. You should be able to trust your lawyer to be your advocate at all times throughout your divorce. The counsel of your attorney can affect your life for years to come. You will never regret taking the time and energy to choose the right one for you. And, importantly, if during the process, you have concerns about your lawyer's advice, you should be able to be open and honest with your attorney to tell that attorney your concerns. Sometimes the advice that your lawyer will give you is not what you want to hear—but that does not mean that it is not the right advice. That requires having a relationship of trust.

See your relationship with your attorney as a partnership for pursuing what is most important to you. With clear and open attorney-client communication, you'll have the best outcome possible and your entire divorce will be less stressful. Don't be afraid to tell your attorney if you don't understand the reasons for the advice he or she is giving you. Your attorney is a professional and should be able to let you know why they are giving you the advice they are. By working closely with the right lawyer, by beginning your relationship with your attorney with open and honest communication, and by not being afraid to express your concerns if you don't understand something, you will have a greater understanding of each step of your divorce.

3.1 Where do I begin looking for an attorney for my divorce?

There are many ways to find a divorce lawyer. The best way is by asking people you trust who have gone through a divorce and have been satisfied with their attorney. If they thought they had a great lawyer (or if their former spouse did), set up a consultation with that attorney to see if you will have the same feeling about that attorney when you meet them.

If you know professionals who work with attorneys, ask for a referral to an attorney who is experienced in family law. Consult your local bar association to find out whether they have a referral service. Be sure to specify that you are looking for an attorney who handles divorces.

Go online. Many attorneys have websites provide information on their practices areas, professional associations, experience, and philosophy.

3.2 How do I choose the right attorney?

Choosing the right attorney for your divorce is an important decision. Your attorney should be a trusted professional with whom you feel comfortable sharing information openly. He or she should be a person you can trust and a zealous advocate for your interests.

You will rely upon your attorney to help you make many decisions throughout the course of your divorce. You will also entrust your legal counsel to make a range of strategic and procedural decisions on your behalf.

Consultation for a divorce might be your first meeting with a lawyer. Know that attorneys want to be supportive and to fully inform you. Feel free to seek all of the information you need to help you feel secure in knowing you have made the right choice.

Find an attorney who practices primarily in family law. While many attorneys do divorces, it is likely you will have more effective representation at a lower cost from an attorney who already knows the fundamentals of divorce law in Florida.

Determine the level of experience you want in your attorney. For example, if you have a short marriage with new children and few assets, an attorney with lesser experience might be a good value for your legal needs. However, if you are anticipating a custody dispute or have complex or substantial assets, a more experienced attorney may better meet your needs.

Consider the qualities in an attorney that are important to you. Even the most experienced and skilled attorney is not right for every client. Ask yourself what it is that you are really looking for in an attorney so you can make your choice with these standards in mind.

It is important that you be confident in the attorney you hire. If you're unsure about whether the lawyer is really listening to you or understanding your concerns, keep looking until you find one who will. Your divorce is an important matter. It's critical that you have a professional you can trust.

3.3   Should I interview more than one attorney?

Be willing to interview more than one attorney. Every lawyer has different strengths and it is important that you find the one that is right for you. Sometimes it is only by meeting with more than one attorney that you see clearly who will best be able to help you reach your goals in the way you want. Sometimes you have to change lawyers in the middle of litigation but it can be stressful and costly. It is wise to invest energy at the outset in making right choice.

3.4   My spouse says since we're still friends we should use the same attorney for the divorce. Is this a good idea?

Even the most amicable of divorcing couples can have differing interests. For this reason, it is never recommended that an attorney represent both parties to a divorce. In most cases, an attorney is ethically prohibited from representing both parties in one divorce, even if both parties agree.

Sometimes couples reach an agreement without understanding all of their rights under the law. A client often will benefit from receiving legal advice on matters such as tax considerations, retirement, and health insurance issues.

It is not uncommon for one party to retain an attorney and for the other party not to do so. In such cases, the party with the attorney files the petition and agreements reached between the parties are typically sent to the spouse for approval prior to any court hearing. If your spouse has filed for divorce and said that you do not need an attorney, you should nevertheless meet with a lawyer before you sign any agreement. The attorney can review the agreement and give you advice about whether you have overlooked or now known about all of your legal rights.

3.5 What information should I take with me to the first meeting with my attorney?

Attorneys differ on the amount of information they like to see at an initial consultation. If a court proceeding, either a divorce or a protection order, has already been initiated by either you or your spouse, it is important to bring copies of any court documents.

If you have a prenuptial or postnuptial agreement with your spouse, that is another important document for you to bring at the outset of your case.

If you intend to ask for support, either for yourself or for children, documents evidencing income of both you and your spouse will also be useful. These might include:

- Recent pay stubs
- Individual and business tax returns, W-2s, and 1099s
- A few months of bank statements
- A statement of your monthly budget can also be helpful.

Your attorney will ask you to complete a questionnaire at the time of your first meeting. Ask whether it is possible to do this in advance of your meeting. This can allow you to provide more complete information and to make the most of your appointment time with the lawyer.

If your situation is urgent or you do not have access to these documents, don't let it stop you from scheduling your appointment with an attorney. Prompt legal advice about your rights is often more important than having detailed financial information in the beginning. Your attorney can explain to you the options for obtaining these financial records if they are not readily available to you.

3.6 What unfamiliar words might an attorney use at the first meeting?

Law has a language all its own, and attorneys sometimes lapse into "legalese," forgetting that non-lawyers may not recognize words used daily in the practice law. Some words and phrases you might hear include:

- *dissolution of marriage*—the divorce
- *petitioner*—person who files the divorce complaint
- *respondent*—person who did not file the divorce complaint
- *jurisdiction*—authority of a court to make rulings affecting a party
- *service*—process of notifying a party about a legal filing
- *discovery*—process during which each side provides information to the other
- *final judgment*—the final order entered in a divorce

Never hesitate to ask your attorney the meaning of a term. Your complete understanding of your lawyer's advice is essential for you to partner with your lawyer as effectively as possible.

3.7 What can I expect at an initial consultation with an attorney?

Most attorneys will ask that you complete a questionnaire prior to the meeting. With few exceptions, attorneys are required to keep confidential all information you provide.

The nature of the advice you get from an attorney in an initial consultation will depend upon whether you are still deciding whether you want a divorce, whether you are planning for a possible divorce in the future, or whether you are ready to file for divorce right away.

During the meeting, you will have an opportunity to provide the following information to the attorney:

- A brief history of the marriage
- Background information regarding yourself, your spouse, and your children
- Your immediate situation
- Your intentions and goals regarding your relationship with your spouse
- What information you are seeking from the attorney during the consultation

You can expect the attorney to provide the following information to you:

- The procedure for divorce in Florida
- A preliminary list of the issues important in your case
- A preliminary assessment of your rights and responsibilities under the law
- Background information regarding the firm
- Information about fees and billings

While some questions may be impossible for the attorney to answer at the initial consultation because additional information or research is needed, the initial consultation is an opportunity for you to ask all of the questions you have at the time of the meeting.

3.8   Can I bring a friend or family member to my initial consultation?

Yes. Having someone present during your initial consultation can be a source of great support. You might ask him or her to take notes on your behalf so that you can focus on listening and asking questions. Remember that this is your consultation, however, and it is important that the attorney hear the facts of your case directly from you.

3.9 What exactly will my attorney do to help me get a divorce?

Your attorney will play a critical role in helping you get your divorce. You will be actively involved in some of the work, while other actions will be taken behind the scenes at the law office, the law library, or the courthouse.

Your attorney may perform any of the following tasks on your behalf:

- Assess the case to determine which court has jurisdiction to hear the matter.
- Develop a strategy for advising you about all aspects of your divorce, including the treatment of assets and matters regarding children.
- Prepare legal documents for filing with the court.
- Conduct discovery to obtain information from the other party, which could include depositions, requests for production of documents, and written interrogatories.
- Appear with you at all court appearances, depositions, and conferences.
- Schedule all deadlines and court appearances.
- Support you in responding to information requests from your spouse.
- Inform you of actions you are required to take.
- Perform financial analyses of your case.
- Conduct legal research.
- Prepare you for court appearances and depositions.
- Prepare your case for hearings and trial, including preparing exhibits and interviewing witnesses.
- Advise you regarding your rights under the law.
- Counsel you regarding the risks and benefits of negotiated settlement as compared to proceeding to trial.

As your advocate, your attorney is entrusted to take all of the steps necessary to represent your interests in the divorce.

3.10 What professionals might the court appoint to work with my attorney?

Sometimes when custody or parenting time issues are disputed, either you or your spouse may ask the court may appoint a *guardian ad litem* to represent the best interest of the child. A guardian *ad litem* has the responsibility to investigate you and your spouse as well as the needs of your child. He or she may then be called as a witness at trial to testify regarding any relevant observations.

Another expert who could be appointed by the court at the request of either party is a *psychologist*. The role of the psychologist will depend upon the purpose for which she or he was appointed. The psychologist may be appointed to perform a parenting evaluation. A *parenting evaluation* involves assessing both the parents and the child. The psychologist could also be ordered to evaluate one parent to access the child's safety while spending time with that parent.

3.11 I've been divorced before and I don't think I need an attorney this time; however, my spouse is hiring one. Is it wise to go it alone?

Having gone through a prior divorce, it's likely that you have learned a great deal about the divorce process as well as your legal rights. However, there are many reasons why you should be extremely cautious about proceeding without legal representation.

It is important to remember that every divorce is different. The length of the marriage, whether there are children, the relative financial situation for you and your spouse, as well as your age and health can all affect the financial outcome in your divorce.

The law may have changed since your last divorce. Some aspects of divorce law are likely to change each year. New laws get passed and new decisions get handed down by the Florida Supreme Court and the Florida Court of Appeals that affect the rights and responsibilities of people who divorce.

In some cases, the involvement of your lawyer could be minimal. This might be the case if your marriage was short, your financial situation very similar to that of your spouse, there are no children, and the two of you remain amicable. At a minimum, have an initial consultation with an attorney to discuss your rights and have an attorney review any final agreement before you sign it.

3.12　Can I take my children to meetings with my attorney?

It's best to make other arrangements for your children when you meet with your attorney. Your attorney will be giving you a great deal of important information during your conferences, and it will benefit you to give your full attention.

It is also recommended that you take every measure to keep information about the legal aspects of your divorce away from your children. Knowledge that you are seeing an attorney can add to your child's anxiety about the process. It can also make your child a target for questioning by the other parent about your contacts with your attorney.

Most law offices are not designed to accommodate young children and are ordinarily not "child-proof." For both your child's well-being and your own peace of mind, explore options for someone to care for your child when you have meetings with your attorney.

3.13　What is the role of the *paralegal* or *legal assistant* in my attorney's office?

A *paralegal,* or *legal assistant,* is a trained legal professional whose duties include providing support for you and your lawyer. Working with a paralegal can make your divorce easier because he or she is likely to be very available to help you. It can also lower your legal costs, as the hourly rate for paralegal services is less than the rate for attorneys.

A paralegal is prohibited from giving legal advice. It is important that you respect the limits of the role of the paralegal if he or she is unable to answer your question because it calls for giving a legal opinion. However, a paralegal can answer many questions and provide a great deal of information to you throughout your divorce.

Paralegals can help you by receiving information from you, reviewing documents with you, providing you with updates on your case, and answering questions about the divorce process that do not call for legal advice.

3.14　My attorney is not returning my phone calls. What can I do?

You have a right to expect your phone calls to be returned by your lawyer. Here are some options to consider:

- Ask to speak to the paralegal or another attorney in the office.

- Send an e-mail or fax telling your lawyer that you have been trying to reach him or her by phone and explaining the reason it is important that you receive a call.

- Ask the receptionist to schedule a phone conference for you to speak with your attorney at a specific date and time.

- Schedule a meeting with your attorney to discuss both the issue needing attention as well as your concerns about the communication.

Your attorney wants to provide good service to you. If your calls are not being returned, take action to get the communication with your lawyer back on track.

3.15   How do I know when it's time to change lawyers?

Changing lawyers is costly. You will incur legal fees for your new attorney to review information which is already familiar to your current attorney. You will spend time giving much of the same information to your new lawyer as the one you have discharged. A change in lawyers often results in delays in the divorce.

The following are questions to ask yourself when you're deciding whether to stay with your attorney or seek new counsel:

- Have I spoken directly to my attorney about my concerns?

- When I expressed concerns, did my lawyer take action accordingly?

- Is my lawyer open and receptive to what I have to say?

- Am I blaming my lawyer for bad behavior of my spouse or opposing counsel?

- Have I provided my lawyer the information needed for taking the next action?

- Does my lawyer have control over the complaints I have, or are they ruled by the law or the judge?

- Is my lawyer keeping promises for completing action on my case?
- Do I trust my lawyer?
- What would be the advantages of changing lawyers when compared to the costs?
- Do I believe my lawyer will support me to achieve the outcome I'm seeking in my divorce?

Every effort should be made to resolve challenges with your attorney. If you have made this effort and the situation remains unchanged, it may be time to switch lawyers.

4

Attorney Fees and Costs

Anytime you make a major investment, you want to know what the cost is going to be and what you are getting for your money. Investing in quality legal representation for your divorce is no different.

The cost of your divorce might be one of your greatest concerns. Because of this, you will want to be an intelligent consumer of legal services. You want quality, but you also want to get the best value for the fees you are paying.

Legal fees for a divorce can be costly and the total expense not always predictable. But there are many actions you can take to control and estimate the cost. Develop a plan early on for how you will finance your divorce. Speak openly with your lawyer about fees from the outset. Learn as much as you can about how you will be charged. Insist on a written fee agreement.

By being informed, aware, and wise, your financial investment in your divorce will be money well spent to protect your future.

4.1 Can I get free legal advice from a lawyer over the phone?

Every law firm has its own policy regarding lawyers talking to people who are not yet clients of the firm. Most questions about your divorce are too complex for a lawyer to give a meaningful answer during a brief phone call.

Questions about your divorce require a complete look at the facts, circumstances, and background of your marriage. To obtain good legal advice, it's best to schedule an initial consultation with a lawyer who handles divorces.

4.2   Will I be charged for initial consultation with a lawyer?
It depends. Some lawyers give free consultations, while others charge a fee. When scheduling your appointment, you should be told the amount of the fee. Payment is ordinarily due at the time of the consultation.

4.3   Will I be expected to give money to the attorney after our first meeting? If so, how much?
Your first meeting with the attorney is considered a consultation. This gives you the opportunity to know if you are comfortable and trust the attorney and the attorney the opportunity to determine is he or she wants to accept your case.

If your attorney charges a consultation fee, you will need to be prepared to pay the consultation fee. If at the meeting you decide to hire the attorney and the attorney agrees to accept your case, you and the attorney will then discuss the required retainer fee.

4.4   What exactly is a *retainer* and how much will mine be?
As mentioned earlier, a *retainer* is a sum paid to your lawyer in advance for services to be performed and costs to be incurred in your divorce. This will either be an amount paid toward a "flat-fee" cost for your divorce, or an advance credit for services that will be charged by the hour.

If your case is accepted by the law firm, expect the attorney to request a retainer following the initial consultation. The amount of the retainer may vary from hundreds of dollars to several thousand dollars, depending upon the nature of your case. Contested custody, divorces involving businesses, or interstate disputes, for example, are all likely to require higher retainers.

Other factors that can affect the amount of the retainer include the nature and number of the disputed issues, the degree of conflict between the parties, and the anticipated overall cost of the litigation.

4.5   I don't have any money and I need a divorce. What are my options?

Two factors to consider in your situation are time and money.

Let's look at money first. If your income is very low and your assets are few, you may be eligible to obtain a divorce and no cost or minimal cost through a local legal aid organization.

These organizations have a screening process for potential clients, as well as limits on the nature of the cases they take. The demand for their services is also usually greater than the number of attorneys available to handle cases. Consequently, if you are eligible for legal services from legal aid, you should anticipate being on a waiting list. In short, if you have very little income and few assets, you are likely to experience some delay in obtaining a lawyer.

4.6   I don't have much money, but I need to get a divorce as quickly as possible. What should I do?

If you have some money and want to a divorce as soon as possible, consider some of these options:

- Borrow the legal fees.
- Charge the legal fees on a low-interest credit card.
- Talk with your attorney about using money held in a joint account with your spouse.
- Find an attorney who will work with you on a monthly payment basis.
- Ask your attorney about your spouse paying for your legal fees.
- Contact the local bar association or the Florida Lawyer Referral and Legal Services.
- Let them know you have some ability to pay and ask for help finding a lawyer who will take your case for a reduced fee.

Even if you do not have the financial resources to proceed with your divorce at this time, consult with an attorney to learn your rights and to develop an action plan for steps you can take between now and the time you are able to proceed.

Often there are measures you can take right away to protect yourself until you have the money to proceed with your divorce.

4.7   Is there anything I can do on my own to get support for my children if I don't have money for a lawyer for a divorce?

Yes. If you need support for your children, contact Florida Department of Revenue for help in obtaining a child support order. Although they cannot help you with matters such as custody or property division, they can pursue support from your spouse for your children. You can visit their website at www. dor.myflorida/childsupport./pages/default.aspx to either apply online or find the address of your local child support office.

4.8   How much does it cost to get a divorce?

The cost of your divorce will depend upon many factors. Some attorneys perform divorces for a flat fee, but most charge by the hour. A flat fee is a fixed amount for the legal services being provided. A flat fee is more likely to be used when there are no children of the marriage and the parties have agreed upon the division of their property and debts. Most Florida attorneys charge by the hour for divorces.

It is important that your discussion of the cost of your divorce begin at your first meeting with your attorney. It is customary for family law attorneys to request a retainer, also known as a *fee advance,* prior to beginning work on your case.

Be sure to ask your attorney what portion, if any, of the retainer is refundable if you do not continue with the case or terminate your relationship with the attorney.

4.9   What are typical hourly rates for a divorce lawyer?

In Florida, the hourly rate can vary significantly depending on where you are seeking the divorce. The rate your attorney charges may depend upon factors such as skills, reputation, experience, and what other attorneys in the area are charging.

If you have a concern about an attorney's hourly rate, but you would like to hire the firm with which the attorney is associated, consider asking to work with an associate attorney in the firm who is likely to charge a lower rate. Associates are attorneys who ordinarily have less experience than the senior partners. However, they often are trained by the senior partners, very experienced, and fully capable of handling your case.

4.10 Can I make payments to my attorney?

Every law firm has its own policies regarding payment arrangements for divorce clients. Often these arrangements are tailored to the specific client. Most attorneys will require a substantial retainer to be paid at the outset of your case. Some attorneys may accept monthly payments in lieu of the retainer. Others may require monthly payments, or request additional retainers as your case progresses. Ask frank questions of your attorney to be clear about your responsibility for payment of legal fees.

4.11 I've been turned down by legal aid. How can I get the money to pay for a lawyer?

There are a number of options to consider when it looks as though you are without funds to pay an attorney.

First, look again. Ask yourself whether you have closely examined all sources of funds readily available to you. Sometimes we have simply overlooked money that we might be able to access with ease.

Next, talk to your family members and friends. Often those close to you are concerned about your future and would be very pleased to support you in your goal of having your rights protected. While this may be uncomfortable to do, remember that most people will appreciate that you trusted them enough to ask for their help. If the retainer is too much money to request from a single individual, consider whether a handful of persons might each be able to contribute a lesser amount to help you reach your goal of hiring a lawyer.

If your case is not urgent, consider developing a plan for saving the money you need to proceed with a divorce. Your attorney may be willing to receive and hold monthly payments until you have paid in an amount sufficient to pay the initial retainer.

Consider taking out a loan or charging your retainer on a credit card.

Under certain circumstances, an attorney might be willing to be paid from the proceeds of a property settlement. If you and your spouse have acquired substantial assets during the marriage, you may be able to find an attorney who will wait to be paid until the assets are divided at the conclusion of the divorce.

4.12 I agreed to pay my attorney a substantial retainer to begin my case. Will I still have to make monthly payments?

Ask your attorney what will be expected of you regarding payments on your account while the divorce is in progress. Clarify whether monthly payments on your account will be expected, whether it is likely that you will be asked to pay additional retainers, and whether the firm charges interest on past-due accounts. Regular payments to your attorney can help you avoid having a tremendously burdensome legal bill at the end of your case.

4.13 My lawyer gave me an estimate of the cost of my divorce and it sounds reasonable. Do I still need a written fee agreement?

Absolutely. Insist upon a written agreement with your attorney. This is essential not only to define the scope of the services for which you have hired your lawyer, but also to ensure that you have clarity about matters such as your attorney's hourly rate, whether you will be billed for certain costs such as copying, and when you can expect to receive statements on your account.

A clear fee agreement reduces the risk of misunderstandings between you and your lawyer. It supports you both to be clear about your promises to one another so that your focus can be on the legal services being provided rather than on disputes about your fees.

4.14 How will I know how the fees and charges are accumulating?

Be sure your written fee agreement with your attorney is completely clear about how you will be informed regarding the status of your account. If your attorney agrees to handle your divorce for a flat fee, your fee agreement should clearly set forth what is included in the fee.

Most attorneys charge by the hour for handling divorces. At the outset of your case, be sure your written fee agreement includes a provision for the attorney to provide you with regular statements of your account. It is reasonable to ask that these be provided monthly.

Review the statement of your account promptly after you receive it. Check to make sure there are no errors, such as duplicate billing entries. If your statement reflects work which you were unaware was performed, call for clarification. Your attorney's office should welcome any questions you have about services it provided.

Your statement might also include filing fees, court reporter fees for transcripts of court testimony or depositions, mediation fees, copy expenses, or interest charged on your account.

If several weeks have passed and you have not received a statement on your account, call your attorney's office to request one. Legal fees can mount quickly, and it is important that you stay aware of the status of your legal expenses.

4.15 What other expenses are related to the divorce litigation besides lawyer fees?

Talk to your attorney about costs other than the attorney fees. Ask whether it is likely there will be filing fees, court reporter expenses, mediation fees, subpoenas, or expert-witness fees. Expert-witness fees can be a substantial expenses ranging from hundreds to thousands of dollars, depending upon the type of expert and the extent to which he or she is involved in your case.

Speak frankly with your attorney about these costs so that together you can make the best decisions about how to use your budget for the litigation.

4.16 Who pays for the experts such as the appraiser, the accountant, and the psychologist?

Costs for the services of experts, whether appointed by the court or hired by the parties, are ordinarily paid for by the parties.

In the case of the guardian *ad litem* who may be appointed to represent the best interest of your children, the amount of the fee will depend upon how much time this professional spends. The judge often orders this fee to be shared by the parties. However, depending upon the circumstances one party can be ordered to pay the entire fee.

Psychologists either charge by the hour or can set a flat fee for a certain type of evaluation. Again, the court can order one party to pay this fee or both parties to share the expense. It is not uncommon for a psychologist to request payment in advance and hold the release of an expert report until fees are paid.

The fees for many experts, including appraisers and accountants, will vary depending upon whether the individuals are called upon to provide only a specific service such as an appraisal, or whether they will need to prepare for giving testimony and appear as a witness at trial.

4.17 What factors will impact how much my divorce will cost?

While it is difficult to predict how much your legal fees will be, the following are some of the factors that affect the cost:

- Whether there are children
- Whether child custody is agreed upon
- Whether there are novel legal questions
- Whether a pension plan will be divided between the parties
- The nature of the issues contested
- The number of issues agreed to by the parties
- The cooperation of the opposing party and opposing counsel
- Whether there are litigation costs, such as fees for expert witnesses or court reporters
- The hourly rate of the attorney

Communicating with your lawyer regularly about your legal fees will help you to have a better understanding of the overall cost as your case proceeds.

4.18   Will my attorney charge for phone calls and e-mails?

Unless your case is being handled on a flat-fee basis, you should expect to be billed for phone calls with your attorney. Many of the professional services provided by lawyers are done by phone and by e-mail. This time can be spent giving legal advice, negotiation, or gathering information to protect your interests. These calls and e-mails are all legal services for which you should anticipate being charged by your attorney.

To make the most of your time during attorney phone calls, plan your call in advance. Organize the information you want to relay, your questions, and any concerns to be addressed. This will help you to be clear and focused during the phone call so that your fees are well spent.

4.19   Will I be charged for talking to the staff at my lawyer's office?

It depends. Check the terms of your fee agreement with your lawyer. Whether you are charged fees for talking to non-lawyer members of the law office may depend upon their role in the office. For example, many law firms charge for the services of paralegals and law clerks.

Remember that non-lawyers cannot give legal advice. Don't expect the receptionist to give you an opinion regarding whether you will win custody or receive alimony.

Your lawyer's support staff will be able relay your messages and receive information from you. They may also be able to answer many of your non-legal questions. Allowing support from non-attorneys in the firm is one way to control your legal fees.

4.20   Can I ask my attorney to develop a budget for legal fees?

If your case is complex and you are anticipating substantial legal fees, ask your attorney to prepare a litigation budget for your review. This can help you to understand the nature of the services anticipated, the time that may be spent, and the overall cost. It can also be helpful for budgeting and planning for additional retainers. Knowing the anticipated costs of litigation can help you to make meaningful decisions about which issues to litigate and which to consider resolving through settlement negotiations.

4.21 What is a *trial retainer* and will I have to pay one?

A *trial retainer* is a sum of money paid on your account with your lawyer when it appears as though your case may not settle and is at risk for proceeding to trial.

The purpose of the trial retainer is to fund the work needed to prepare for trial and for services the day or days of trial.

Confirm with your attorney that any unearned portion of you trial retainer will be refunded if you case settles. Ask your lawyer whether and when a trial retainer might be required in your case so that you can avoid surprise and plan your budget accordingly.

4.22 How do I know whether I should spend the attorney fees my lawyer says it will take to take my case to trial?

Deciding whether to take a case to trial or to settle is often the most challenging point in the divorce process. This decision should be made with the support of your attorney.

When the issues in dispute are primarily financial, often the decision about settlement is related to the costs of going to trial. Decide just how far apart you and your spouse are on the financial matters and compare this to the estimated costs of going to trial. By comparing these amounts, you can decide whether a compromise on certain financial issues and certainty about the outcome would be better than paying legal fees and not knowing how your case will resolve.

4.23 If someone helps to pays my legal fees, will my lawyer give him/her private information about my divorce?

If someone other than you is paying your legal bills, it is important that you be clear with your lawyer and with the person paying that you expect your lawyer to honor the ethical duty to maintain confidentiality. Without your permission, your attorney should not be disclosing information to others about your case unless you consent to it.

If you do want your lawyer to be able to communicate with your family members or friends who are helping pay, advise your lawyer. Expect to be charged by your lawyer for the time spent on these calls or meetings. Regardless of the opinions of the person who pays your attorney fees, your lawyer's duty is to remain your zealous advocate.

4.24 Can I ask the court to order my spouse to pay my attorney fees?

Yes. If you want to ask the court to order your spouse to pay any portion of your legal fees, be sure to discuss this with your attorney at the first opportunity. Most lawyers will treat the obligation for your legal fees as yours until the other party has made payment.

If your case is likely to require costly experts and your spouse has a much greater ability to pay these expenses than you, talk to your lawyer about the possibility of filing a motion with the court asking your spouse to pay toward these costs while the case is pending.

4.25 What happens if I don't pay my attorney the fees I promised to pay?

The ethical rules for lawyers allow your attorney to withdraw from representation if you do not comply with your fee agreement. Consequently, it is important that you keep the promises you have made regarding your account.

If you are having difficulty paying your attorney's fees, talk with your attorney about payment options. Consider borrowing the funds, using your credit card, or asking for help from friends and family.

Above all, do not avoid communication with your attorney if you are having challenges making payment. Keeping in touch with your attorney is essential for you to have an advocate at all stages of your divorce.

4.26 Is there any way I can reduce some of the expenses of getting a divorce?

Litigation of any kind can be expensive, and divorces are no exception. The good news is that there are many ways that you can help to control the expense. Here are some of them.

Put it in writing. If you need to relay information that is important but not urgent, consider providing to your attorney it by mail, fax, or e-mail. This creates a prompt and accurate record for your file and your lawyer's in less time than exchanging phone messages and talking on the phone.

Keep your attorney informed. Just as your attorney should keep you up to date on the status of your case, you need you to do the same. Keep your lawyer advised about any major developments in your life such as plans to move, to have someone move into your home, to change your employment status, or to buy or sell property.

During a divorce, your address, phone number, or e-mail address may change. Be sure to let your attorney know. Often timely advice on the part of your lawyer can avoid the need for more costly fees later.

Obtain copies of documents. An important part of litigation includes reviewing documents such as tax returns, account statements, report cards, or medical records. Your attorney will ordinarily be able to request or subpoena these items, but many may be readily available to you directly upon request.

Utilize support professionals. Get to know the support staff at your lawyer's office. The receptionist, paralegal, legal secretary, or law clerk may be the person who has the answer to your question. Only the attorneys in the office are able to give you legal advice, but other professionals in the law office can often provide the answers to questions regarding the status of your case. Just as your communication with your attorney, all communication with any professionals in a law firm is required to be kept strictly confidential.

Consider working with an associate attorney. Although the senior attorneys or partners in a law firm may have more experience, you may find that working with the associate attorney is a good option. Hourly rates for an associate attorney are typically lower than those charged by a senior partner. Frequently the associate attorney has trained under a senior partner and developed excellent skills as well as the knowledge of the law. Many associate attorneys are also very experienced.

Discuss with the firm the benefits of working with a senior or an associate attorney in light of the nature of your case, the expertise of the respective attorneys, and the potential cost savings to you.

Leave a detailed message. If your attorney knows the information you are seeking, she or he can often get the answer before returning your call. This not only gets your answer faster, but also reduces costs.

Discuss more than one matter during a call. It is not unusual for clients to have many questions during litigation. If your question is not urgent, consider waiting to call until you have more than one inquiry. Never hesitate to call to ask any legal questions.

Provide timely responses to information request. Whenever possible, provide information requested by your lawyer in a timely manner. This avoids the cost of follow-up action by your lawyer and the additional expense of extending the time in litigation.

Carefully review your monthly statements. Scrutinize your monthly billing statements closely. If you believe an error has been made, contact your lawyer's office right away to discuss your concerns.

Remain open to settlement. Be alert to when your disagreement is about smaller sums of money that will cost more in legal fees to take to court than the value of what is disputed. By doing your part, you can use your legal fees wisely and control the costs of your divorce.

5

The Discovery Process

Interrogatories. Depositions. *Subpoena duces tecum.* Even the words sound foreign. Discovery is one of the least talked about steps in divorce, but it is often among the most important. The discovery process enables you and your spouse to meet on a more level playing field when it comes to settling your case or taking it to trial.

You and your spouse both need the same information if you hope to reach agreement on any of the issues in your divorce. Similarly, the judge must know all of the facts to make a fair decision. The purpose of discovery is to ensure that both you and your spouse have access to the same information. In this way, you can either negotiate a fair agreement or have all of the facts and documents to present to the judge at trial.

The discovery process may seem tedious at times because of the need to obtain and to provide lots of detailed information. Completing it, however, can give tremendous clarity about the issues in your divorce. Trust your lawyer's advice about the importance of having the necessary evidence as you complete the discovery process in order to reach your goals in your divorce.

5.1 What is *discovery?*

Discovery is that part of your divorce process in which the attorneys attempt to learn as much about the facts of your case as possible. Through a variety of methods, both lawyers will request information from you, your spouse, and potential witnesses in your case.

5.2 Is there any mandatory discovery that the court requires?

Yes. Both you and your spouse are required to complete a *financial affidavit* and provide certain "mandatory disclosure" documents. A financial affidavit is completed using a form provided by your attorney. In addition, the court requires both parties to provide specific documents, for example, income records, bank statements, credit card statement, and other documents evidencing marital debts.

5.3 What additional types of discovery might be done by my lawyer or my spouse's lawyer?

Types of discovery include:

- *Interrogatories,* which are written questions that must be answered under oath
- *Requests for production of documents,* asking that certain documents be provided by you or your spouse
- Requests for *admissions,* asking that certain facts be admitted or denied
- Subpoena of documents
- *Depositions* in which questions are asked and answered in the presence of a court reporter but outside of the presence of a judge

Factors that can influence the type of discovery conducted in your divorce can include:

- The types of issues in dispute
- How much access you and your spouse have to needed information
- The level of cooperation in sharing information
- The budget available for performing discovery

Talk to your lawyer about the nature and extent of discovery anticipated in your case.

5.4 How long does the discovery process take?

Discovery can take anywhere from a few weeks to a number of months, depending upon factors such as the complexity of the case, the cooperation of you and your spouse, and whether expert witnesses are involved.

The *Florida Rules of Discovery* provide that interrogatories, requests for production of documents, and requests for admissions be responded to within thirty days.

5.5 My lawyer insists that we conduct discovery, but I don't want to spend the time and money on it. Is it really necessary?

The discovery process can be critical to a successful outcome in your case for several reasons:

- It increases the likelihood that any agreements reached are based upon accurate information.
- It provides necessary information for deciding whether to settle or proceed to trial.
- It supports the preparation of defenses by providing information regarding your spouse's case.
- It avoids surprises at trial, such as unexpected witness testimony.

Discuss with your attorney the intention behind the discovery being conducted in your case to ensure it is consistent with your goals and a meaningful investment of your legal fees.

5.6 I just received from my spouse's attorney interrogatories and requests that I produce documents. My lawyer wants me to respond within two weeks. I'll never make the deadline. What can I do?

Answering your discovery promptly will help move your case forward and help control your legal fees. There are steps you can take to make this task easier.

First, look at all of the questions. Many of them will not apply or your answers will be a simple "yes" or "no."

Ask a friend to help you. It is important that you develop the practice of letting others help you while you are going through your divorce. Chances are that you will make great progress in just a couple of hours with a friend helping you.

Break it down into smaller tasks. If you answer just a few questions a day, the job will not be so overwhelming.

Call your lawyer. Ask whether a paralegal in the office can help you organize the needed information or determine whether some of it can be provided at a later date.

Delay in the discovery process often leads to frustration by clients and lawyers. Do your best to provide the information in a timely manner with the help of others.

5.7 My spouse's lawyer intends to subpoena my medical records. Aren't these private?

Whether or not your medical records are relevant in your case will depend upon the issues in dispute. If you are requesting alimony or if your health is an issue in the dispute of child custody, these records may be relevant.

Talk with your lawyer about your rights. It may be that a motion to stop the subpoena, known as a *motion to quash* or *motion for protective order* is needed, or that the nature of the records which can be obtained should be limited to those relevant to your divorce.

5.8 It's been two months since my lawyer sent interrogatories to my spouse, and we still don't have his answers. I answered mine on time. Is there anything that can be done to speed up the process?

The failure or refusal of a spouse to follow the rules of discovery can add to both the frustration and expense of the divorce process.

Talk with your attorney about filing a *motion to compel,* seeking a court order that your spouse provides the requested information by a certain date. A request for attorney fees for the filing of the motion may also be appropriate.

Ask your lawyer whether a subpoena of information from an employer or a financial institution would be a more cost effective way to get needed facts and documents if your spouse remains uncooperative.

5.9 What is a *deposition?*

A *deposition* is the asking and answering of questions under oath, outside of court, in the presence of a court reporter. A deposition may be taken of you, your spouse, or potential witnesses in your divorce case, including experts. Both attorneys will be present. You and your spouse also have the right to be present during the taking of depositions of any witnesses in your case.

Depositions are not performed in every divorce. They are most common in cases involving contested custody, complex financial issues, and expert witnesses.

After your deposition is completed, the questions and answers will be transcribed, that is, typed, by the court reporter exactly as given and bound into one or more volumes.

5.10   What is the purpose of a deposition?

A deposition can serve a number of purposes, such as:

- Supporting the settlement process by providing valuable information
- Helping your attorney determine who to use as witnesses at trial
- Aiding in the assessment of a witness's credibility, that is, whether the witness appears to be telling the truth
- Helping avoid surprise at trial by learning the testimony of witnesses in advance
- Preserving testimony in the event the witness becomes unavailable for trial

Depositions can be essential tools in a divorce, especially when a case is likely to proceed to trial.

5.11   Will what I say in my deposition be used against me when we go to court?

Usually, deposition is used to develop trial strategy and obtain information in preparation for trial. In some circumstances, a deposition may be used at trial.

If you are later called to testify as a witness and give testimony contrary to your deposition, your deposition can be used to impeach you by showing the inconsistency in your statements. It is important to review your deposition prior to your live testimony to ensure consistency and prepare yourself for the type of questions you may be asked.

5.12   Will the judge read the depositions?

Unless a witness becomes unavailable for trial or gives conflicting testimony at trial, it is unlikely that the judge will ever read the depositions.

5.13   How should I prepare for my deposition?

To prepare for your deposition, review the important documents in your case such as the complaint, your answers to interrogatories, and your financial affidavit.

Gather all documents you've been asked to provide at your deposition. Deliver them to your attorney in advance of your deposition for copying and review. Talk to your attorney about the type of questions you can expect to be asked. Discuss with him or her any questions you are concerned about answering.

5.14   What will I be asked? Can I refuse to answer questions?

Questions in a deposition can cover a broad range of topics including your education, work, income, and family. The attorney is allowed to ask anything that is reasonably calculated to lead to the discovery of admissible evidence. If the question may lead to relevant information, it can be asked in a deposition, even though it may be inadmissible at trial. If you are unsure whether to answer a question, ask your lawyer and follow his or her advice.

Your attorney also may object to inappropriate questions. If there is an objection, say nothing until the attorneys discuss the objection. You will be directed whether or not to answer.

5.15   What if I give incorrect information in my deposition?

You will be under oath during your deposition, so it is very important that you be truthful. If you give incorrect information by mistake, contact your attorney as soon as you realize the error. If you lie during your deposition, you risk being impeached during by the other lawyer during your divorce trial. This could cause you to lose credibility with the court, rendering your testimony less valuable.

5.16   What if I don't know or can't remember the answer to a question?

You may be asked questions about which you have no knowledge. It is always acceptable to say "I don't know" if you do not have the knowledge. Similarly, if you cannot remember, simply say so. It is important not to guess as this can later be used as an inconsistent statement if you later remember.

5.17 What else do I need to know about having my deposition taken?

The following suggestions will help you to give a successful deposition:

- Prepare for your deposition by reviewing and providing necessary documents and talking with your lawyer.

- Get a good night's sleep the night before. Eat a meal with protein to sustain your energy, as the length of depositions can vary.

- Arrive early for your deposition so that you have time to get comfortable with your surroundings.

- Relax. You are going to be asked questions about matters you know about. Your deposition is likely to begin with routine matters such as your educational and work history.

- Tell the truth, including whether you have met with an attorney or discussed preparation for the deposition.

- Stay calm. Your spouse's lawyer will be judging is your credibility and demeanor. Do not argue with the attorneys.

- Listen carefully to the entire question. Do not try to anticipate questions or start thinking about your answer before the attorney has finished asking the question.

- Answer the question directly. If the question calls only for "yes" or "no," provide such an answer.

- Do not volunteer information. If the lawyer wants to elicit more information, he or she will do so in following questions.

- If you do not understand the question clearly, ask that it be repeated or rephrased. Do not try to answer what you think was asked.

- Take your time and carefully consider the question before answering. There is no need to hurry.

- If you do not know or cannot remember the answer, say so. That is an adequate answer.

- Do not guess.

- If your answer is an estimate or approximation, say so. Do not let an attorney pin you down to anything you are not sure about. For example, if you cannot remember the number of times an event occurred, say that. If the attorney asks you if it was more than ten times, answer only if you can. If you can provide a range (more than ten but less than twenty) with reasonable certainty, you may do so.

- If an attorney mischaracterizes something you said earlier, say so.

- Speak clearly and loudly enough for everyone to hear you.

- Answer all questions with words, rather than gestures or sounds. "Uh-huh"is difficult for the court reporter to distinguish from "unh-unh" and may result in inaccuracies in the transcript.

- If you need a break at any point in the deposition, you have a right to request one. You can talk to your attorney during such a break.

- Discuss with your lawyer in advance of your deposition whether you should review the transcript of your deposition for its accuracy or whether you should waive your right to review and sign the deposition.

- Remember that the purpose of your deposition is to support a good outcome in your case. Completing it will help your case to move forward.

5.18 Are depositions always necessary? Does every witness have to be deposed?

Depositions are less likely to be needed if you and your spouse are reaching agreement on most of the facts in your case and you are moving toward a settlement. They are more likely to be needed in cases where child custody is disputed or where there are complex financial issues. Although depositions of all witnesses are usually unnecessary, it is common to take to the depositions of expert witnesses.

5.19   Will I get a copy of the depositions in my case?

Ask your attorney for copies of the depositions in your case. It will be important for you to carefully review your deposition if your case proceeds to trial.

6

Mediation and Negotiation

If your marriage was full of conflict, you might be asking how you can make the fighting stop. You picture your divorce looking like a scene from the movie *War of the Roses,* (which if you haven't seen, you really should) complete with vicious lawyers and screaming matches. You wonder if there is a way out of this nightmare.

Or, perhaps you and your spouse are parting ways amicably. While you are in disagreement about how your divorce should be settled, you are clear you want the process to be respectful and without hostility. You'd rather spend your hard earned money on your children's college education than legal fees.

In either case, going to trial and having a judge make all of the decisions in your divorce is not inevitable. In fact, most Florida divorce cases settle without the need for a trial.

Mediation and negotiation can help you and your spouse resolve your disputed issues without taking your case before the judge who will make your decisions for you. You reach your own agreements rather than allowing the court to make them for you.

Resolving your divorce through a mediated or negotiated settlement has many advantages. You can achieve a mutually satisfying agreement, a known outcome, little risk of appeal, and often enjoy significantly lower legal fees. Despite the circumstances which led to the end of your marriage, it might be possible for your divorce to conclude peacefully with the help of these tools.

6.1 What is the difference between *mediation* and *negotiation*?

Both mediation and negotiation are methods used to help you and your spouse settle your divorce by reaching an agreement rather than going to trial and having the judge make decisions for you.

Mediation uses a trained mediator who is an independent, neutral third party. He or she is a skilled professional who can assist you and your spouse in the process. *Negotiation* involves lawyers for both you and your spouse. Lawyers for the spouses will also be present during mediation, although their involvement is usually less than in negotiation.

6.2 How are mediation and negotiation different from a *collaborative divorce*?

Collaborative law is a method of resolving a divorce case where both parties have a strong commitment to settling their disputes and avoiding litigation. You and your spouse each hire an attorney trained in the collaborative law process. You and your lawyers enter into an agreement which provides that, in the event either you or your spouse decides to take the case to court, both of you must terminate services with your collaborative lawyers and start anew.

Often spouses in the collaborative process enlist the support of other professionals, such as an independent financial advisor or coaches, to support them through the process. While the process may be lengthy, it enables the focus to shift away from the conflict and toward finding solutions. The attorneys become a part of the team supporting settlement rather than advocates adding to the conflict.

Talk to your lawyer about whether your case would be well suited to the collaborative law process.

6.3 What is involved in the mediation process? What will I have to do and how long will it take?

Mediation is the opportunity for you and your spouse to come up with an agreement that resolves some or all of the issues of your divorce. The process is confidential to allow everyone to have more open discussions and not fear that what you say will be used against you in court if you do not settle.

Should you proceed to court, the judge will only know whether you did or did not settle.

The mediator will outline ground rules designed to ensure you will be treated respectfully and given an opportunity to be heard. The attorneys will have an opportunity to provide a summary of the issues to the mediator. The mediator will attempt to help facilitate options and ideas to assist in resolving the issues.

How long the process of mediation continues depends upon many of the same factors that affect how long your divorce will take. These include how many issues you and your spouse disagree about, the complexity of these issues, and the willingness of each of you to work toward an agreement.

Your case could settle after just one mediation session or it might require a series of meetings. It is common for the mediator to clarify at the close of the session whether the parties are willing to continue with another session.

6.4   My lawyer said that mediation and negotiation can reduce delays in completing my divorce. How does this work?

When the issues in your divorce are decided by a judge instead of by you and your spouse, there are many opportunities for delay. These can include:

- Waiting for a trial date
- Having to return to court on a later, second date if your trial is not completed on the day it is scheduled
- Waiting for the judge's ruling on your case
- Additional court hearings after your trial to resolve disputes about the intention of your judge's rulings, issues that were overlooked, or disagreement regarding language of the decree

Each one of these events holds the possibility of delaying your divorce by days, weeks, or even months. Mediating or negotiating the terms of your divorce decree can eliminate these delays.

6.5 How can mediation and negotiation lower the costs of my divorce?

If your case is not settled by agreement, you will be going to trial. If the issues in your case are many or if they are complex, such as custody, the attorney's fees and other costs of going to trial can be tremendous.

By settling your case without going to trial, you may be able to save thousands of dollars in legal fees. Ask your attorney for a litigation budget that sets forth the potential costs of going to trial, so that you have some idea of these costs when deciding whether to settle an issue or to take it to trial before the judge.

6.6 Are there other benefits to mediating or negotiating a settlement?

Yes. A divorce resolved by a mediated or negotiated agreement can have these additional benefits:

Recognizing common goals. Mediation and negotiation allow for brainstorming between the parties and lawyers. Looking at all possible solutions, even the impractical ones, invites creative solutions to common goals. For example, suppose you and your spouse both agree that you need to pay your spouse some amount of equity for the family home you will keep, but you have no cash to make the payment. Together, you might come up with a number of options for accomplishing your goal and select the best one. Contrast this with the judge who simply orders you to pay the money without considering all of the possible options.

Addressing the unique circumstances of your situation. Rather than using a one-size-fits-all approach as a judge might do, a settlement reached by agreement allows you and your spouse to consider the unique circumstances of your situation in formulating a good outcome. For example, suppose you disagree about the parenting times for the Thanksgiving holiday. The judge might order you to alternate the holiday each year, even though you both would have preferred to have your child share the day.

Creating a safe place for communication. Mediation and negotiation give each party an opportunity to be heard. Perhaps you and your spouse have not yet had an opportunity to share directly your concerns about settlement. For example, you might be worried about how the temporary parenting time arrangement is impacting your children, but have not yet talked to your spouse about it. A mediation session or settlement conference can be a safe place for you and your spouse to communicate your concerns about your children or your finances.

Fulfilling your children's needs. You may see that your children would be better served by you and your spouse deciding their future rather than by a judge who does not know, love, and understand your children like the two of you do.

Eliminating the risk and uncertainty of trial. If a judge decides the outcome of your divorce, you give up control over the terms of the settlement. The decisions are left in the hands of the judge. If you and your spouse reach agreement, however, you have the power eliminate the risk of an uncertain outcome.

Reducing the risk of harm to your children. If your case goes to trial, it is likely that you and your spouse will give testimony that will be upsetting to each other. As the conflict increases, the relationship between you and your spouse inevitably deteriorates. This can be harmful to your children. Contrast this with mediation or settlement negotiations, in which you open your communication and seek to reach agreement. It is not unusual for the relationship between the parents to improve as the professionals create a safe environment for rebuilding communication and reaching agreements in the best interest of a child.

Having the support of professionals. Using trained professionals such as mediators and lawyers to support you can help you to reach a settlement that you might think is impossible. These professionals have skills to help you and focus on what is most important to you, shift your attention away from irrelevant facts. They understand the law and know the possible outcomes if your case goes to trial.

Lowering stress. The process of preparing for and going to court can be stressful. Your energy is going toward caring for your children, looking at your finances, and coping with the emotions of divorce. You might decide that you would be better served by settling your case rather than proceeding to trial.

Achieving closure. When you are going through a divorce, the process can feel as though it is taking an eternity. By reaching agreement, you and your spouse are better able to put the divorce behind you and move forward with your lives.

6.7   Is mediation mandatory?

In most jurisdictions, mediation is mandatory before the court will proceed to trial. Check with your attorney to determine whether it is mandatory in your county.

6.8   What if I want to try mediation and my spouse doesn't?

Because mediation is most likely mandatory, your spouse does not have an option. If it is not mandatory, your attorney can file a motion to request the judge order mediation.

6.9   My spouse abused me and I am afraid to participate in mediation. Should I participate anyway?

If the court in your county requires mediation, talk to your attorney about whether it is possible to file a motion for the court to waive mediation.

If you have to proceed to mediation, your attorney can require that you and your spouse are not in the same room. Talk to your attorney about having the mediation at your lawyer's office, where you feel more comfortable.

Also have your attorney insist on a mediator that has a good understanding of the dynamics of domestic abuse and how they can impact the mediation process.

6.10   What training and credentials do mediators have?

The background of mediators varies. Some are attorneys; many come from other backgrounds such as counseling. Some mediators have received their training through the state of Florida; others were trained out of state. Ask your attorney for help in finding a qualified mediator who has completed training in mediating family law cases. The availability of mediators also varies depending upon where you live.

6.11   What types of issues can be mediated or negotiated?

All of the issues in your case are to be mediated or negotiated.

Talk with your lawyer in advance of any mediation about custody to be absolutely clear about the impact of the parenting schedule on child support. Agreeing to certain parenting schedules can drastically reduce child support, and you should not negotiate on parenting time without having first fully discussed your attorney its impact on child support.

You may decide that certain issues are nonnegotiable for you. Discuss this with your attorney in advance of any mediation or negotiation sessions so that he or she can support you in focusing the discussions on the issues you are open to looking at.

6.12 What is the role of my attorney in the mediation process?

The role of your attorney in the mediation process is to assist in facilitating a satisfactory agreement by making sure you understand your legal rights and the strengths and weaknesses in your case.

6.13 How do I prepare for mediation?

Prior to attending a mediation session with your spouse, discuss with your attorney the issues and your limitations on settlement of each issue. Enlist your attorney's support in identifying your intentions for the mediation. Make a list of the issues important to you. For example, when it comes to your child, you might consider whether it is your child's safety, the parenting time schedule, or the ability to attend your children's events which concerns you more.

Be forward looking. Giving thought to your desired outcomes while approaching mediation with an open mind and heart is the best way to move closer to settlement.

6.14 Do children attend the mediation sessions?

No. Mediation is an opportunity for you and your spouse to resolve the matter without involving the children.

6.15 Does my attorney have to attend the mediation?

No, however, if there are complicated issues, it is advisable that your attorney attend with you. It is generally expected that your attorney will attend the mediation with you, therefore, it is important to make sure opposing counsel and the mediator will agree to you appearing on your own behalf.

6.16 I went to mediation without an attorney and I want my attorney to look over the agreement before I give my final approval. Is this possible?

Yes. Before giving your written or final approval to any agreements reached in mediation, it is critical that your attorney review the agreement first. This is necessary to ensure that you understand the terms of the settlement and its implications. Your attorney will also review the agreement for compliance with Florida law.

6.17 Who pays for mediation?

The cost of mediation must be paid for by you or your spouse. Often it is a shared expense. Expect your mediator to address the matter of fees before or prior to the beginning of the mediation session.

6.18 What if mediation fails?

If mediation is not successful, you still may be able to settle your case through negotiations between the attorneys. Also, you and your spouse can agree to preserve the settlements that were reached and to take only the remaining disputed issues to the judge for trial.

6.19 What is a *settlement conference*?

A *settlement conference* can be a powerful tool for the resolution of your case. It is a meeting held with you, your spouse, and your lawyers with the intention of negotiating the terms of your divorce. In some cases, a professional with important information needed to support the settlement process, such as an accountant, may also participate.

Settlement conferences are most effective when both parties and their attorneys see the potential for a negotiated resolution and have the necessary information to accomplish that goal.

6.20 Why should I consider a settlement conference when the attorneys can negotiate through letters and phone calls?

A settlement conference can eliminate the delays which often occur when negotiation takes place through correspondence and calls between the attorneys. Rather than waiting days or weeks for a response, you can receive a response on a proposal in a matter of minutes.

A settlement conference also enables you and your spouse, if you choose, to use your own words to explain the reasoning behind your requests. You are also able to provide information immediately to expedite the process.

6.21 How do I prepare for my settlement conference?

Being well prepared for the settlement conference can help you make the most of this opportunity to resolve your case without the need to go to trial. Actions you should take include:

- Provide in advance of the conference, all necessary information. If your attorney has asked for a current pay stub, tax return, debt amounts, asset values, or other documentation, make sure it is provided prior to the meeting.

- Discuss your topics of concern with your attorney in advance. Your lawyer can assist you in understanding your rights under the law so that you can have realistic expectations for the outcome of negotiations.

- Bring a positive attitude, a listening ear, and an open mind. Come with the attitude that your case will settle. Be willing to first listen to the opposing party, and then to share your position. To encourage your spouse to listen to your position, listen to hers or his first. Resist the urge to interrupt.

Few cases settle without each side demonstrating flexibility and a willingness to compromise. Most cases settle when the parties are able to bring these qualities to the process.

6.22   What will happen at my settlement conference?

Typically, the conference will be held at the office of one of the attorneys, with both parties and lawyers present. If there are a number of issues to be discussed, an agenda may be used to keep the focus on relevant topics. From time to time throughout the conference, you and your attorney may meet alone to consult as needed. If additional information is needed to reach agreement, some issues may be set aside for later discussion.

The length of the conference depends upon the number of issues to be resolved, the complexity of the issues, and the willingness of the parties and lawyers to communicate effectively. An effort is made to confirm which issues are resolved and which issues remain disputed. Then, one by one the issues are addressed.

6.23   What is the role of my attorney in the settlement conference?

Your attorney is your advocate during the settlement conference. You can count on him or her to support you throughout the process, to see that important issues are addressed, and to counsel you privately outside of the presence of your spouse and his or her lawyer.

6.24   Why is my lawyer appearing so friendly with my spouse and her lawyer?

Successful negotiations rely upon building trust between the parties working toward agreement. Your lawyer may be respectful or pleasant toward your spouse or your spouse's lawyer to promote a good outcome for you.

6.25   What happens if my spouse and I settled some but not all of the issues in our divorce?

You and your spouse can agree to maintain the agreements you have reached and let the judge decide those matters which you are unable to resolve.

6.26 If my spouse and I reach an agreement, how long will it take before the divorce is final?

If a settlement is reached through negotiation or mediation, one of the attorneys will put the agreement in writing for approval by you and your spouse. In most cases, a final judgment can be entered by the judge within thirty days.

7

Emergency:
When You Fear a Spouse

Suddenly you are in a panic. Maybe your spouse was serious when he said he'd take your child and leave the state. What if you're kicked out of your own home? Suppose all of the bank accounts are emptied? Your fear heightens as your mind spins with all of the possibilities from every horror story you ever heard about divorce.

Facing an emergency situation in divorce can feel as though your entire life is at stake. You may not be able to concentrate on anything else. At the same time, you may be paralyzed with anxiety and have no idea how to begin to protect yourself. No doubt you have countless worries about what your future holds.

Remember that you have overcome many challenges in your life before this moment. There are people willing to help you. You have strength and wisdom you may not yet even realize. Step by step, you will make it through this time.

When facing an emergency, do your best to focus on what to do in the immediate moment. Set aside your worries about the future for another day. Now it is time to stay in the present moment, let others support you, and start taking action right away.

7.1   My spouse has deserted me, and I need to get divorced as quickly as possible. What is my first step?

Your first step is to get legal advice as soon as possible. The earlier you get legal counsel to advise you about your rights, the better. The initial consultation will answer most of your questions and start you on an action plan for getting your divorce underway.

7.2 I'm afraid my abusive spouse will try to hurt me and/or our children if I say I want a divorce. What can I do legally to protect myself and my children?

Develop a plan with your safety and that of your children as your highest priority. In addition to meeting with an attorney at your first opportunity, develop a safety plan in the event you and your children need to escape your home. A great way to do this is to let in support from an agency that helps victims of domestic violence. Call the Florida Domestic Violence Hotline at (800) 500-1119 or go their website at www.fcadv.org to get more information about the domestic violence program closest to you.

Your risk of harm from an abusive spouse can increase when you leave. For this reason, all actions must be taken with safety as the first concern.

Find a lawyer who understands domestic violence. Often your local domestic violence agency can help with a referral. Talk to your lawyer about the concerns for your safety and that of your children. Ask your lawyer about an *injunction for protection against domestic violence.* Your lawyer can talk to you about whether the violence you may have experienced or are in fear of meets the standard for having an order of protection granted. This is a court order which may offer a number of protections including granting you temporary custody of your children and ordering your spouse to leave the family residence and have no contact with you.

7.3 I am afraid to meet with a lawyer because I am terrified my spouse will find out and get violent. What should I do?

Schedule an initial consultation with an attorney who is experienced in working with domestic violence victims. When you schedule the appointment, let the firm know your situation and instruct the law office not to place any calls to you which you think your spouse might discover.

Consultations with your attorney are confidential. Your lawyer has an ethical duty to not disclose your meeting with anyone outside of the law firm. Let your attorney know your concerns so that extra precautions can be taken by the law office in handling your file.

7.4   I want to give my attorney all the information needed so my children and I are safe from my spouse. What does this include?

Provide your attorney with complete information about the history, background, and nature, and evidence of your abuse including:

- The types of abuse (for example, physical, sexual, verbal, financial, mental, emotional)
- The dates, time frames, or occasions
- The locations
- Whether you were ever treated medically
- Any police reports made
- E-mails, letters, notes, or journal entries
- Any photographs taken
- Any witnesses to the abuse or evidence of the abuse
- Any statements made by your spouse admitting the abuse
- Any damaged property
- Injuries you or your children suffered
- Abuse of family pets
- Any counseling you had because of the abuse
- Alcohol or drug abuse
- The presence of guns or other weapons

The better the information you provide to your lawyer, the easier it will be for him or her to make a strong case for the protection of you and your children.

7.5   I'm not ready to hire a lawyer for a divorce, but I am afraid my spouse is going to get violent with my children and me in the meantime. What can I do?

It is possible to seek an injunction for protection against domestic violence from the court without an attorney. It is possible for the judge to order your spouse out of your home, granting you custody of your children and order your spouse to stay away from you.

7.6 What's the difference between a *protection order* and a *restraining order?*

Protection orders and restraining orders are both court orders directing a person to not engage in certain behavior. Both of them are intended to protect others. While either can initially be obtained without notice to the other person, there is always a right to a hearing to determine whether a protection order or restraining order should remain in place.

Talk to your attorney about obtaining a *protection order* if you are concerned about the safety of you children or yourself or if there has been a history of domestic violence. The violation of a protection order is a criminal offense which can result in immediate arrest.

If you are concerned that your spouse will annoy, threaten, harass, or intimidate you after your divorce complaint is filed, ask your lawyer about a *restraining order*. If your spouse violates the restraining order, he or she may be brought before the court for contempt.

7.7 My spouse has never been violent, but I know she is going to be really angry and upset when the divorce papers are served. Do I need a protection order?

The facts of your case may not warrant a protection order. However, if you are still concerned about your spouse's behavior, ask your attorney about a temporary restraining order which can be requested in the divorce petition. This court order would direct your spouse not to annoy, threaten, intimidate, or harass you while the divorce is in progress. A temporary restraining order can also order your spouse not to sell or transfer assets until your divorce is completed.

7.8 My spouse says I am crazy, that I am a liar, and that no judge will ever believe me if I tell the truth about the abusive behavior. What can I do if I don't have any proof?

Most domestic violence is not witnessed by third parties. Often there is little physical evidence. Even without physical evidence, a judge can enter orders to protect you and your children if you give truthful testimony about your abuse which the judge finds believable. Your own testimony of your abuse is evidence.

It is very common for persons who abuse others to claim that their victims are liars and to make statements intended to discourage disclosure of the abuse. This is yet another form of controlling behavior.

Your attorney's skills and experience will support you to give effective testimony in the courtroom to establish your case. Let your lawyer know your concerns so that a strong case can be presented to the judge based upon your persuasive statements of the truth of your experience.

7.9 I'm afraid my spouse is going to take all of the money out of the bank accounts and leave me with nothing. What can I do?

Talk to your attorney immediately. If you are worried about your spouse emptying financial accounts or selling marital assets, it is critical that you take action at once. Your attorney can advise on your right to take possession of certain assets in order to protect them from being hidden or spent by your spouse.

Ask your lawyer about seeking a *temporary restraining order (TRO)*. This order forbids your spouse to sell, transfer, hide, or otherwise dispose of marital property until the divorce is complete.

A temporary restraining order is intended to prevent assets from "disappearing" before a final division of the property from your marriage is complete.

If this is a concern of yours, talk to your lawyer about the benefits of obtaining a temporary restraining order as to property prior to giving your spouse notice of that you are filing for divorce.

7.10 My spouse told me that if I ever file for divorce, I'll never see my child again. Should I be worried about my child being abducted?

Your fear that your spouse will abduct your children is a common one. It can be helpful to look at some of the factors that appear to increase the risk that your child will be removed from the state by the other parent.

Programming and brainwashing are almost always present in cases where a child is at risk for being kidnapped by a parent, and efforts to isolate the child may also be seen. Exit activities such as obtaining a new passport, getting financial matters in order, or contacting a moving company could be indicators.

Talk to your lawyer to assess the risks in your particular case. Together you can determine whether statements by your spouse are threats intended to control or intimidate you or whether legal action is needed to protect or child.

7.11 What legal steps can be taken to prevent my spouse from removing our child from the state?

If you are concerned about your child being removed from the state, talk to your lawyer about whether any of these options might be available in your case:

* A court order giving you immediate custody until a temporary custody hearing can be held.
* A court order directing your spouse to turn over passports for the child and your spouse to the court.
* The posting of a bond prior to your spouse exercising parenting time
* Supervised visitation

Both state and federal laws are designed to provide protection from the removal of children from one state to another when a custody matter is brought and to protect children from kidnapping. *The Uniform Child Custody Jurisdiction Enforcement Act (UCCJEA)* was passed to encourage the custody of children to be decided in the state where they have been living most recently and where they have the most ties. *The Parental Kidnapping Prevention Act (PKPA)* makes it a federal crime for a parent to kidnap a child in violation of a valid custody order.

If you are concerned about your child being abducted, talk with your lawyer about all options available to you for your child's protection.

7.12 How quickly can I get a divorce in Florida?

There are a number of time requirements for getting a divorce in Florida. Either you or your spouse must have been a resident of Florida for at least six months immediately prior to the filing of the complaint for the divorce with the court. After you file your divorce, your spouse must be given notice of the divorce.

A twenty-one-day waiting period is required for every Florida divorce. This period begins on either the date the date your spouse is served with the divorce petition or the date that a voluntary appearance signed by your spouse is filed with the court.

The soonest a final hearing can be held is after the twenty-one-day waiting period, although most cases do not resolve this quickly. The length of time your case remains pending depends in large part upon the extent to which you and your spouse reach agreement on the issues in your case.

Once a final hearing or trial is held and the judge signs your divorce decree, it becomes final.

7.13 I really need a divorce quickly. Will the divorce I get in another country be valid in Florida?

In order for a divorce from a foreign country to be valid in Florida, several requirements must be met, including, notice to your spouse, proper jurisdiction over you or your spouse, and the order has to comply with the public policy of Florida.

7.14 If either my spouse or I file for divorce, will I be ordered out of my home? Who decides who gets to live in the house while we go through the divorce?

If you and your spouse cannot reach agreement regarding which of you will leave the residence during the divorce, the judge will decide whether one of you should be granted exclusive possession of the home until the case is concluded. In most cases judges have been known to refuse to order either party out of the house until the divorce is concluded.

Abusive behavior is one basis for seeking temporary possession of the home. If there are minor children, the custodial parent will ordinarily be awarded temporary possession of the residence.

Other factors the judge may consider include:

- Whether one of you owned the home prior to the marriage
- After provisions are made for payment of temporary support, who can afford to remain in the home or obtain other housing
- Who is most likely to be awarded the home in the divorce
- Options available to each of you for other temporary housing, including other homes or family members who live in the area
- Special needs that would make a move unduly burdensome, such as a health condition
- Self-employment from home, which could not be readily moved, such as a child care business

If staying in the home is important to you, talk to your attorney about your reasons so that a strong case can be made for you at the temporary hearing.

8

Parental Responsibility
and Time-Sharing
(Parenting Plans)

Ever since you and your spouse began talking about divorce, chances are your children have been your greatest concern. You or your spouse might have postponed the decision to seek divorce because of concern about the impact on your children. Now that the time has come, you might still have doubts about whether your children will be all right after the divorce.

Remember that you have been making wise and loving decisions for your children since they were born. You've always done your best to see that they had everything they really needed. You loved them and protected them. This won't change simply because you are going through your divorce. You were a good parent before the divorce and you will be a good parent after the divorce.

It can be difficult not to worry about how the sharing of parenting time with your spouse will affect your children. You may also have fears about being cut out of your child's life. Try to remember, it is likely that the court order will not only give you a lot of time with your children but also a generous opportunity to be involved in their day-to-day lives.

With the help of your lawyer, you can make sound decisions regarding a parenting plan and time-sharing schedule that is in the best interest of your children.

8.1   What types of custody are awarded in Florida?
The Florida family laws specifically do not make a designation of "custody" of a child; rather the courts require a *par-*

enting plan that sets forth each parent's responsibility for making major decisions affecting the children and a *time-sharing schedule* detailing when the children will spend time with each parent. The court can order sole parental responsibility, shared parental responsibility, or shared parental responsibility with one parent have ultimate decision making authority for some or all decisions affecting the children.

If you have *sole parental responsibility,* you are responsible for making all major decisions affecting the children, such as who their health care providers are and what school they will attend. The other parent may or may not have parenting time, including supervised parenting time or supervised exchanges.

Shared parental responsibility means that you and your former spouse will share equally in the decision making for your child. This means that you and the other parent are required to discuss major decisions affecting the children and come to an agreement about those decisions. If you and the other parent are unable to reach agreement, you may need to return to mediation or to court for the decision to be made by a judge.

There are times the court will award *shared parental responsibility with one parent having the ultimate decision making over certain decisions.* This means that the parent with ultimate decisions making will still have an obligation to inform and discuss with other parent before exercising his or her decision making. The burden then shifts to the other parent to go to court if he or she disagrees with decision.

The courts will generally award shared parental responsibility unless you can prove that it is not in the children's best interest. The Florida legislature has determined that it is presumed to be in the best interest of the children for both parents to play an active role in the lives of the children.

8.2 What is a *parenting plan?*

A *parenting plan* is a detailed document that sets out the responsibilities of each parent toward each other and the children, defines each parents' role in decision making for the children, sets out each parents' financial responsibilities in regard to costs for extracurricular activities, travel, and any other children's expenses not related to child support, and includes the time-sharing schedule. The parenting plan should also include provisions for the following:

- Phone access to the child
- Communication regarding the child
- Access to records regarding the child
- Notice regarding parenting time
- Attendance at the child's activities
- Decision-making regarding the child
- Travelling with the child
- Financial responsibility for each parent for extracurricular activities
- Exchange of information such as addresses, phone numbers, and care providers

The time-sharing portion of the parenting plan will include a detailed schedule for each parent to spend time with the children, including days of the week, school breaks, summer, holidays, and vacations. The plan can also include supervised time-sharing or supervised exchanges if there are safety concerns.

The parenting plan can either be agreed to between the parents or, if they can not agree, the court will order a specific parenting plan.

8.3 How does the court determine what is in the best interest of the children?

Florida statutes have set out the many factors that the judge considers when establishing a parenting plan. The judge will consider all relevant evidence to determine what is in "the best interest of the child." Specifically, the judges are required use the following factors as set forth in *Florida Statutes 61.13:*

- The demonstrated capacity and disposition of each parent to facilitate and encourage a close and continuing parent-child relationship, to hone the time-sharing schedule, and to be reasonable when changes are required.

- The anticipated division of parental responsibilities after the litigation, including the extent to which parental responsibilities will be delegated to third parties.
- The demonstrated capacity and disposition of each parent to determine, consider, and act upon the needs of the child as opposed to the needs or desires of the parent.
- The length of time the child has lived in a stable, satisfactory environment and the desirability of maintaining continuity.
- The geographic viability of the parenting plan, with special attention paid to the needs of school-age children and the amount of time to be spent traveling to effectuate the parenting plan. The factor does not create a presumption for or against relocation of either parent with a child.
- The moral fitness of the parents.
- The home, school, and community record of the child.
- The reasonable preference of the child, if the court deems the child to be of sufficient intelligence, understanding, and experience to express a preference.
- The demonstrated knowledge, capacity, and disposition of each parent to be informed of the circumstances of the minor child, including, but not limited to the child's friends, teachers, medical care providers, daily activities, and favorite things.
- The demonstrated capacity and disposition of each parent to provide a consistent routine for the child, such as discipline, and daily schedules for homework, meals, and bedtime.
- The demonstrated capacity of each parent to communicate with and keep informed the other parent of issues and activities regarding the minor child, and the willingness of each parent to adopt a unified front on all major issues when dealing with the child.
- Evidence of domestic violence, sexual violence, child abuse, child abandonment, or child neglect, regardless of whether a prior or pending action relating to

those issues has been brought. If the court adopts evidence of prior of pending actions regarding domestic violence, sexual violence, child abuse, child abandonment, or child neglect, the court must specifically acknowledge in writing the such evidence was considered with evaluating the best interest of the child.

- Evidence that either parent has knowingly provided false information to the court regarding any prior or pending action regarding domestic violence, sexual violence, child abuse, child abandonment, or child neglect.

- The particular parenting tasks customarily performed by each parent and the division of parental responsibilities before the institution of litigation and during the pending litigation, including the extent to which parenting responsibilities were undertaken by third parties.

- The demonstrated capacity and disposition of each parent to participate and be involved in the child's school and extracurricular activities.

- The demonstrated capacity and disposition of each parent to maintain an environment for the child which is free from substance abuse.

- The capacity and disposition of each parent to protect the child from the ongoing litigation as demonstrated by not discussing the litigation with the child, not sharing documents or electronic media related to the litigation with the child, and refraining from disparaging comments about the other parent to the child.

- The developmental stages and needs of the child and the demonstrated capacity and disposition of each parent to meet the child's developmental needs.

- Any other factor that is relevant to the determination of a specific parenting plan, including the time-sharing schedule.

8.4   What's the difference between *visitation* and *parenting time?*

Historically, time spent with the noncustodial parent was referred to as *visitation*. Today, the term *parenting time* is used to refer to the time a child spends with either parent.

This change in language reflects the intention that children spend time with both parents and have two homes, as opposed to their living with one parent and visiting the other.

8.5   How do I make sure I have time with my children during the divorce proceedings?

A temporary parenting plan with a time-sharing schedule is the best way to be sure you have time with your children while your divorce is proceeding. Even if you and your spouse have agreed to temporary arrangements, talk with your attorney about whether this agreement should be formalized in a court order so that it can be enforced.

Obtaining a temporary order can be an important protection not only for the temporary issues affecting your children, but for other issues such as support and temporary exclusive possession of the marital home.

Until a temporary order is entered, it is best that you communicate with your spouse regarding your children, including time-sharing. It is usually recommended that the children have as little disruption in their lives as possible. If you must leave your home and take your children with you talk with your attorney about seeking the appropriate court orders. These might include orders for protection against domestic violence, a temporary time-sharing schedule, support, possession of your home, or attorney fees.

8.6   How much weight does the child's preference carry?

The preference of your child is only one of many factors a judge considers in determining an appropriate parenting plan. Although there is no age at which your child's preference is the determining factor, most judges give more weight to the wishes of an older child.

The reasoning underlying your child's preference is also a factor to consider. Consider the fifteen-year-old girl who wants to live with her mother because "Mom lets me stay out past curfew, I get a bigger allowance, and I don't have to do chores." Greater weight might be given to the preference of an eight-year-old who wants to live with his mother because "she helps me with my homework, reads me bedtime stories, and doesn't call me names like Dad does."

If you see that your child's preference may be a factor in the determination of a parenting schedule, discuss it with your lawyer so that this consideration is a part of assessing the action to be taken in your case.

8.7 Does it matter that I was the primary care provider during the marriage?

In general, the courts will be more concerned about what has happened since you and your spouse separated because it is more indicative of how you will parent from this point forward.

8.8 Do I have to let my spouse see the children before we are actually divorced?

Unless your children are at risk for being harmed by your spouse, your children should maintain regular contact with the other parent.

It is important for children to experience the presence of both parents in their lives, regardless of the separation of the parents. Even if there is no temporary order for parenting time, cooperate with your spouse in making reasonable arrangements for time with your children.

When safety is not an issue, if you deny contact with the other parent prior to trial, your judge is likely to question whether you have the best interest of your child at heart. Talk to your spouse or your lawyer about what parenting time schedule would be best for your children on a temporary basis.

8.9 I am seeing a therapist. Will that impact the judge's decision when ordering a parenting plan?

If you are seeing a therapist, acknowledge yourself for getting the professional support you need. Your well-being is important to your ability to be the best parent you can be.

Talk over with your lawyer the implications of your being treated by a therapist. It may be that the condition for which you are being treated in no way affects your child or your ability to be a loving and supportive parent.

Your mental health records may be subpoenaed by the other parent's lawyer. For this reason, it is important to discuss with your attorney an action plan for responding to a request to obtain records in your therapist's file. Ask your attorney to contact your therapist to alert him or her regarding how to respond to a request for your mental health records.

8.10   Can having a live-in partner hurt my chances of getting parenting time?

If you are contemplating having your partner live with you, discuss your decision with your attorney first. If you are already living with your partner, let your attorney know right away so that the potential impact on any parenting issues can be assessed.

Your living with someone who is not your spouse may have significant impact on the court's parenting plan decisions. However, judges' opinions of the significance of this factor can vary greatly. Talk promptly and frankly with your lawyer. It will be important for you to look together at many aspects, including the following:

- How the judge assigned to your case views this situation
- Whether your living arrangement is likely to prompt a dispute over the children that would otherwise not arise
- How long you have been separated from the other parent
- How long you have been in a relationship with your new partner
- The history and nature of the children's relationship with your partner
- Your future plans with your partner (such as marriage)

8.11   Will all the sordid details of my or my spouse's affair have to come out in court in front of the children?

Judges make every effort to protect children from the conflict of their parents. Most likely your children will never be in the courtroom. In the event they are brought to court to testify, most judges will not allow children to be present in the courtroom to hear the testimony of other witnesses.

While the risk that your spouse may share information with your child cannot be eliminated, it would be highly unusual for a judge to allow a child to hear such testimony in a courtroom.

8.12 Should I hire a private investigator to prove my spouse is having an affair?

It depends. If parenting issues are disputed and your spouse is having an affair, discuss with your attorney how a private investigator might help you gather evidence to support your case. Discuss the following considerations with your attorney:

- What view on extramarital relationships does my judge hold?
- How is the affair affecting the children?
- How much will a private investigator cost?
- Will the evidence gathered help my case?

Your attorney can help you determine whether hiring a private investigator is a good idea in your particular case.

8.13 Will the fact that I had an affair during the marriage affect the court's decisions regarding the children?

Whether a past affair will have any impact on your custody case will depend upon many factors, including:

- The views of the judge assigned to your case
- Whether the affair had any impact on the children
- How long ago the affair occurred
- The quality of the evidence about the affair

If you had an affair during your marriage, discuss it with your attorney at the outset so that you can discuss its impact, if any, on the children's issues.

8.14   During the months it takes to get a divorce, is it okay to date or will it affect the court's decisions regarding the parenting plan?

If children's issues are disputed, talk with your attorney about your plans to begin dating. Your dating may be irrelevant if the children are unaware of it. However, most judges will frown upon exposing your children to a new relationship when they are still adjusting to the separation of their parents.

If your spouse is contesting the children's issues, you may see that it would be best to focus your energy on your children, the litigation, and taking care of yourself.

If you do date and become sexually involved with your new partner, it is imperative that your children not be exposed to any sexual activity. If they are, it could impact the judge's decisions in ordering a parenting plan.

8.15   I'm gay and came out to my spouse when I filed for divorce. What impact will my sexual orientation have on my case for custody or parenting time?

There are no laws in Florida that limit your rights as a parent based upon your sexual orientation. Social science research shows that gay and lesbian parents are more similar than dissimilar to heterosexual parents.

Exposing your child to sexual activity or engaging in sexual activity which harms your child are relevant factors in a contested dispute involving the children. However, your sexual orientation is not the same as your sexual activity.

Be sure to choose a lawyer whom you have confidence will fully support you in your goals as a parent. Understand that, to dispel certain myths, you may need to educate your spouse, opposing counsel, and the judge.

8.16   How is *abandonment* legally defined, and how might it affect the outcome of our custody battle?

Abandonment is rarely an issue in family law litigation unless one parent has been absent from the child's life for an extended period.

Under Florida law, *abandonment* is determined by the facts and circumstances of each case. It must have occurred for a significant period of time and be without a just case or excuse. The intentional absence of a parent's presence, care, protection, and support are all considered.

Where abandonment has occurred for an extended period of time a court may consider terminating parental rights, but only if doing so would be in the best interest of the child.

8.17 Can I have witnesses speak on my behalf for the court's determination of a parenting plan?

Absolutely. Witnesses are critical in every case involving children. The witness will generally have to appear in person at the hearings or trial. The court will not accept a written affidavit in lieu of live testimony.

Among those you might consider as potential witnesses in your custody case are:

- Family members
- Family friends
- Child-care providers
- Neighbors
- Teachers
- Health-care providers
- Clergy members

In considering which witnesses would best support your case, your attorney may consider the following:

- What has been this witness's opportunity to observe you or the other parent, especially with your child. How frequently? How recently?
- How long has the witness known you or the other parent?
- What is the relationship of the witness to the child and the parents?
- How valuable is the knowledge that this witness has?
- Does this witness have knowledge different from that of other witnesses?
- Is the witness available and willing to testify?
- Is the witness clear in conveying information?
- Is the witness credible, that is, will the judge believe this witness?

- Does the witness have any biases or prejudices that could impact the testimony?

You and your attorney can work together to determine which witnesses will best support your case. Support your attorney by providing a list of potential witnesses together with your opinion regarding the answers to the above questions.

Give your attorney the phone numbers, addresses, and work places of each of your potential witnesses. This information can be critical for the role that the attorney has in interviewing the witnesses, contacting them regarding testifying, and issuing subpoenas to compel their court attendance if needed. When parents give conflicting testimony during a trial, the testimony of other witnesses can be key to determining the outcome of the case.

8.18   How old do the children have to be before they can speak to the judge about whom they want to live with?

It depends upon the judge. There is no set age at which children are allowed to speak to the judge about their preferences as to time-sharing.

If either you or your spouse want to have the judge listen to what your child has to say, a request is ordinarily made to the judge to have the child speak to the judge in the judge's office (chambers) rather than from the witness stand. Depending upon the judge's decision, the attorneys for your and your spouse may also be present.

It is possible that the judge may also allow the attorneys to question the child. If you have concerns about the other parent learning what your child says to the judge, talk to your lawyer about the possibility of obtaining a court order keep this information from the other parent.

Typically, the testimony of the child is made "on the record," that is, in the presence of a court reporter. This is so that the testimony can be transcribed later in the event of an appeal.

In addition to the age of a child, a judge may consider such facts as the child's maturity and personality in determining whether an *in camera* interview of the child by the judge will be helpful to the custody decision-making process.

8.19 Will my attorney want to speak with my children?

It is generally not appropriate for your attorney to speak with the children. Your attorney is your attorney and not the child's attorney. Especially if there is a dispute regarding the parenting issues, you nor your attorney want to even appear to have influenced the children or involved the children in the litigation. If your children are insistent about talking to the judge or an attorney, you can request an attorney *ad litem* or guardian *ad litem* be appointed for the children.

8.20 What is a *guardian ad litem?* Why is one appointed?

In family law cases, a *guardian ad litem* is an individual who may be appointed by the court to represent the best interest of the child. The guardian *ad litem,* sometimes referred to as the *GAL,* is directed by the judge to conduct an investigation on the issues in dispute.

The guardian *ad litem* may be called as a witness by you or your spouse to give testimony of her or his knowledge, based upon the investigation. For example, he or she might testify regarding the unsafe housing conditions of a parent. In some cases, the attorneys may agree that a written report prepared by the guardian *ad litem* be received into evidence for the judge's consideration.

8.21 How might a DVD or video taken from my phone of my child help my custody case?

A movie of your child's day-to-day life can help the judge learn more about your child's needs. It can demonstrate how your child interacts with you, siblings, and other important people in your family's life. The judge can see your child's room, home, and neighborhood.

Talk to your lawyer about whether a video or DVD would be helpful in your case. Such a video should show routines in your child's day, including challenging moments such as bedtime or disciplining.

If your lawyer recommends making a video talk with him or her about what scenes to include, the length of the video, keeping the original media, and the editing process.

8.22 Why might I not be awarded *shared parental responsibility?*

You will not be awarded *shared parental responsibility* if the judge determines that you are not able to make decisions in the bests interest of your children.

Determinations of your ability to make shared parental decisions in the best interest of your child will largely depend upon the facts of your case. Reasons why a parent might be found to be unable to participate in decision making include a history of physical abuse, alcohol or drug abuse, or mental health problems which affect the ability to parent. A judge's ruling on the best interest of a child is based upon numerous factors.

A decision by the judge that your spouse should have sole parental responsibility does not require a conclusion that you are an unfit parent. Even if the judge determines that both you and your spouse are fit to have custody, he or she may nevertheless decide that it is in the best interest of your child that only one of you be awarded sole parental responsibility.

8.23 Does shared parental responsibility always mean equal time at each parent's house?

No. Shared parental responsibility does not determine what the time-sharing scheduled will be and does not necessarily mean an equal division of parenting time. Remember, parental responsibility and time-sharing are two separate issues.

Whether it is sole or shared parental responsibility, you and your spouse can agree to share parenting time in a way that best serves your children. An example would be where you and you spouse agree to shared parental responsibility, but the majority of the parenting time will be with one parent.

It can also be helpful to remember that day-to-day decisions, such as a child's daily routine, will usually be made by the parent who has the child that day.

8.24 What are some of the risks of shared parental responsibility?

Shared parental responsibility may be a good idea when the parents agree to it, they have been separated for a period of time and have been able to reach decisions regarding their children without the involvement of attorneys or the court, and where the other factors for shared parental responsibility are present.

Shared parental responsibility requires healthy communication between you and your spouse. Without it, you are at risk for conflict, stress, and delay when making important decisions for your child. If communication with your spouse regarding your child is poor, think carefully before agreeing to shared parental responsibility.

If you share parental responsibility and are unable to reach agreement on a major decision, such as a child's school or child-care provider, you and your former spouse may be required to return to mediation or to court to resolve your dispute. This can lead to delays in decision-making for matters important to your child, increased conflict, and legal fees.

8.25 If my spouse has sole parental responsibility of my child, will I still have parenting time with our children?

Parenting time schedules vary from case to case. As in the determination of parental responsibility, the best interest of the child are what a court considers in determining the parenting time schedule. Among the factors which can impact a parenting time schedule are the past history of parenting time, the age and needs of the child, and the parents' work schedules.

If you and your spouse are willing to reach your own agreement about the parenting time schedule, you are likely to be more satisfied with it than one imposed by a judge. Because the two of you know your child's needs, your family traditions, and your personal preferences, you can design a plan uniquely suited to your child's best interest.

If you and your spouse are unable to reach an agreement on a parenting time schedule, either on your own or with the assistance of your lawyers or a mediator, the judge will decide the schedule.

8.26 Is there a standard parenting time schedule that the court's use?

No. Parenting time schedules are generally at the discretion of the court although Florida courts do presume that children have the right to have substantial time sharing with both parents.

8.27 I don't think it's safe for my children to have any contact with my spouse. How can I prove this to the judge?

Keeping your children safe is so important that this discussion with your attorney requires immediate attention. Talk with your attorney about a plan for the protection of you and your children. Options might include a protection order, supervised visitation, or certain restrictions on your spouse's parenting time.

Make sure you have an attorney who understands your concerns for the welfare of your children. If your attorney is not taking your worry about the safety of your children seriously, you may be better served by a lawyer with a greater understanding of the issues in your case.

Give your attorney a complete history of the facts upon which you base your belief that your children are not safe with the other parent. While the most recent facts are often the most relevant, it is important that your attorney have a clear picture of the background as well.

Your attorney also needs information about your spouse, such as whether your spouse is or has been:

- Using alcohol or drugs
- Treated for alcohol or drug use
- Arrested, charged, or convicted of crimes of violence
- In possession of firearms
- Subject to a protection order for harassment or violence

8.28 My spouse keeps saying he'll get "custody" because there were no witnesses to his abuse and I can't prove it. Is he right?

No. Most domestic violence is not witnessed by others, and judges know this.

If you have been a victim of abusive behavior by your spouse, or if you have witnessed your children as victims, your testimony is likely to be the most compelling evidence.

Be sure to tell your attorney about anyone who may have either seen your spouse's behavior or spoken to you or your children right after an abusive incident. They may be important witnesses in your case.

8.29 I am concerned about protecting my children from abuse by my spouse. Which types of past abuse by my spouse are important to tell my attorney?

Keeping your child safe is your top priority. So that your attorney can help you protect your child, give him or her a full history of the following:

- Hitting, kicking, pushing, shoving, or slapping you or your child
- Sexual abuse
- Threats harm to you or the child
- Threatened to abduct your child
- Destruction of property
- Torture or other harm to pets
- Requiring your child to keep secrets

The process of writing down past events may help you to remember other incidents of abuse that you had forgotten. Be as complete as possible.

8.30 What documents or items should I give my attorney to help prove the history of domestic violence by my spouse?

The following may be useful exhibits if your case goes to court:

- Photographs of injuries
- Photographs of damaged property
- Abusive or threatening notes, letters, or e-mails
- Abusive or threatening voice messages
- Your journal entries about abuse
- Police reports
- Medical records
- Court records
- Criminal and traffic records

- Damaged property, such as torn clothing

Discuss with your attorney any of these that you are able to obtain and ask your lawyer whether others can be acquired through a subpoena or other means.

8.31 How can I get the other parent's parenting time to be supervised?

If you are concerned about the safety of your children when they are with the other parent, talk to your lawyer. It may be that a protection order is warranted to terminate or limit contact with your children. Alternatively, it is possible to ask the judge to consider certain court orders intended to better protect your children.

Ask your attorney whether, under the facts of your case, the judge would consider any of the following court orders:

- Supervised visits
- Exchanges at a child protection agency
- Exchanges of the children in a public place
- Parenting class for the other parent
- Psychological evaluation
- Drug and alcohol evaluation
- Anger management, batter's intervention, or other rehabilitative program for the other parent
- A prohibition against drinking by the other parent when with the children

Judges have differing approaches to cases where children are at risk. Recognize that there are also often practical considerations, such as cost or the availability of people to supervise visits. Urge your attorney to advocate zealously for court orders to protect your children from harm by the other parent.

8.32 I want to talk to my spouse about our child, but all she wants to do is argue. How can I communicate without it always turning into a fight?

Because conflict is high between you and your spouse, consider the following:

- Ask your lawyer to help you obtain a court order for parental responsibility and parenting time that is specific and detailed. This lowers the amount of necessary communication between you and your spouse.

- Put as much information in writing as possible. Consider asking the court to order you both to use www. Familywizard.com for scheduling and information exchange.
- Consider using e-mail, mail, or fax, especially for less urgent communication.
- Avoid criticisms of your spouse's parenting.
- Avoid directing your spouse regarding how to parent.
- Be factual, concise, and business-like.
- Acknowledge to your spouse the good parental qualities he or she displays, such as being concerned, attentive, or generous.
- Keep your child out of any conflicts.

By focusing on your behavior, conflict with your spouse has the potential to decrease.

8.33   What if the child is not returned from parenting time at the agreed upon time? Should I call the police?

Calling the police should be done only as a last resort if you feel that your child is at risk for abuse or neglect, or if you have been advised by your attorney that such a call is warranted. The involvement of law enforcement officials in parental conflict can result in far greater trauma to a child than a late return at the end of a parenting time.

The appropriate response to a child not being returned according to a court order depends upon the circumstances. If the problem is a recurring one, talk to your attorney regarding your options. It may be that a change in the schedule would be in the best interest of your child.

Regardless of the behavior of the other parent, make every effort to keep your child out of any conflicts between the adults. In many cases, law enforcement may determine that this is a civil matter that should be resolved by the court and may decline to get involved or enforce any orders without specific instructions from the court to do so.

8.34 If I have sole parental responsibility, can I move without the permission of the court?

Even if you have sole parental responsibility, you must obtain permission of the court prior to moving more than fifty miles from your residence at the time of the last court order. If your former spouse agrees to your move, contact your attorney for preparing and submitting the necessary documents to your former spouse and the court for approval.

If your former spouse objects to your move, you must petition to the court for permission to move, give your spouse notice of the petition, and have a court hearing for the judge to decide if the relocation is in the best interest of your child.

8.35 What factors does the court consider when determining if relocation is in the best interest of the child?

To obtain the court's permission, the court is required to use the following factors to determine if the move is in the best interest of the children:

- The nature, quality, extent of involvement, and duration of the child's relationship with the parent or other person proposing to relocate with the child and with the non-relocating parent, other persons, siblings, half-siblings, and other significant persons in the child's life.

- The age and developmental stage of the child, the needs of the child, and the likely impact the relocation will have on the child's physical, educational, and emotional development, taking into consideration any special needs of the child.

- The feasibility of preserving the relationship between the nonrelocating parent or other person and the child through substitute arrangements that take into consideration the logistics of contact, access, and time-sharing, as well as the financial circumstances of the parties; whether those factors are sufficient to foster a continuing meaningful relationship between the child and the nonrelocating parent or other person; and the likelihood of compliance with the substitute arrangements by the relocating parent or other person once he or she is out of the jurisdiction of the court.

- The child's preference, taking into consideration the age and maturity of the child.
- Whether the relocation will enhance the general quality of life for both the parent or other person seeking the relocation and the child, including, but not limited to, financial or emotional benefits or educational opportunities.
- The reasons each parent or other person is seeking or opposing the relocation.
- The current employment and economic circumstances of each parent or other person and whether the proposed relocation is necessary to improve the economic circumstances of the parent or other person seeking relocation of the child.
- That the relocation is sought in good faith and the extent to which the objecting parent has fulfilled his or her financial obligations to the parent or other person seeking relocation, including child support, spousal support, and marital property and marital debt obligations.
- The career and other opportunities available to the objecting parent or other person if the relocation occurs.
- A history of substance abuse or domestic violence or which meets the criteria of *Florida statute, s. 39.806(1) (d)*, by either parent, including a consideration of the severity of such conduct and the failure or success of any attempts at rehabilitation.
- Any other factor affecting the best interest of the child

8.36 After the divorce, can my spouse legally take our children out of the state during parenting time? Out of the country?

It depends upon the terms of the court order as set forth in your decree.

If you are concerned about your children being out of Florida with the other parent, discuss the possibility of some of these decree provisions regarding out-of-state travel with your child:

- Limits on the duration or distance for out-of-state travel with the child
- Notice requirements
- Information on phone numbers
- Information on physical addresses
- E-mail address contact information
- Possession of the child's passport with the court
- Posting of bond by the other parent prior to travel
- Requiring a court order for travel outside of the country

Although judges are not ordinarily concerned about short trips across state lines, you should let your attorney know if you are concerned that your child may be abducted by the other parent so that reasonable safeguards may be put in place.

8.37 If my spouse was awarded sole parental responsibility, what rights do I have regarding medical records and medical treatment for my child?

If your former spouse has sole parental responsibility, your former spouse would have to agree to provide those documents unless your final judgment allows you access to these documents.

8.38 If I do not have parental responsibility, how will I know what's going on at my child's school? What rights to records do I have there?

Develop a relationship with your child's teachers and the school staff. Request to be put on the school's mailing list for all notices.

Communicate with the other parent to both share and receive information about your child's progress in school. This will enable you to support your child and one another through any challenging periods of your child's education. It also enables you to share a mutual pride in your child's successes.

8.39 What if my child does not want to go for his or her parenting time? Can my former spouse force the child to go?

If your child is resisting going with the other parent, it can first be helpful to determine the underlying reason. Consider these questions:

- What is your child's stated reason for not wanting to go?
- Does your child appear afraid, anxious, or sad?
- Do you have any concerns regarding your child's safety while with the other parent?
- Have you prepared your child for being with the other parent, speaking about the experience with enthusiasm and encouragement?
- Is it possible your child is perceiving your anxiety about the situation and is consequently having the same reaction?
- Have you provided support for your child's transition to the other home, such as completing fun activities in your home well in advance of the other parent's starting time for parenting?
- Have you spoken to the other parent about your child's behavior?
- Can you provide anything that will make your child's time with the other parent more comfortable, such as a favorite toy or blanket?
- Have you established clear routines that support your child to be ready to go with the other parent with ease, such as packing a back pack or saying good-bye to a family pet?

The reason for a child's reluctance to go with the other parent may be as simple as being sad about leaving you or as serious as being a victim of abuse in the other parent's home. It is important to look at this closely to determine the best response.

Judges treat compliance with court orders for parenting time seriously. If one parent believes that the other is intentionally interfering with parenting time or the parent-child relationship, it can result in further litigation. At the same time, you want to know that your child is safe. Talk with your attorney about the best approach in your situation.

8.40 What steps can I take to prevent my spouse from getting the children in the event of my death?

Unless the other parent is not fit to parent the children, your spouse or former spouse will be given the first priority to have "custody" of your child in the event of your death.

All parents should have a will naming a guardian for their children. In the event you do not intend to name the other parent, talk with your attorney. Seek counsel about how to best document and preserve the evidence that will be needed to prove that the other parent is unfit to have custody in the event of your death.

9

Child Support

Whether you will be paying child support or receiving it, it is often the subject of much worry. Will I receive enough support to take care of my children? Will I have enough money to live on after I pay my child support? How will I make ends meet?

All parents want to provide for their children. Today, the child support laws make it possible for parents to having a better understanding of their obligation to support their children. The mechanisms for both payment and receipt of child support are more clearly defined, and help is available for collecting support if it's not paid.

9.1   What determines whether I will get child support?

Florida requires that child support be determined prior to the entry of a divorce. The child support guidelines are used to calculate which parent will pay support based upon net income and the specific time-sharing schedule.

9.2   Can I request child support even if I do not meet the six-month residency requirement for a divorce in Florida?

Yes. Even though you may not have met the requirements to obtain a divorce, you have a right to seek support for your children. Talk to your attorney or visit the Florida Department of Revenue Child Support Office website at http.dor.myflorida.com for a listing of the local offices that can assist you in applying for child support. You can also call (800) 622-KIDS (5437) to speak with a representative.

9.3 Can I get temporary support while waiting for the divorce is still going on?

A judge has authority to enter a temporary order for time-sharing and child support. This order ordinarily remains in place until a final parenting plan and child support order is entered. In most cases a hearing for temporary time-sharing and support can be held shortly after the filing of the petition for divorce.

9.4 What is *temporary support* and how soon can I get it?

Temporary support is paid for the support of a spouse or a child. It is paid sometime after the divorce petition is filed and continues until your final decree of divorce is entered by the court or until your case is dismissed.

If you are in need of temporary support, talk to your attorney at your first opportunity. If you and your spouse are unable to agree upon the amount of temporary support to be paid each month, talk to your attorney. If an agreement is not reached, it is likely that your attorney will file a motion for temporary support asking the judge to decide how much the support should be and when it will start.

Because there are a number of steps to getting a temporary child support order, don't delay in discussing your need for support with your lawyer. Child support will not be ordered for any period prior to the filing of a request for it with the court.

The following are the common steps in the process:

- You discuss your need for a temporary child support order with your lawyer.
- Your lawyer requests a hearing date from the judge and prepares the necessary documents.
- A temporary hearing is held.
- The temporary order is signed by the judge.
- If the court orders the support to be paid by income deduction order, the support payments will be automatically taken from your spouse's paycheck.

- Your spouse's employer sends the support to either clerk of court of the Florida State Disbursement Center.
- The Florida State Disbursement Center sends the money to you.

If your spouse is not paying you support voluntarily, time is of the essence in obtaining a temporary order for support. This should be one of the first issues you discuss with your lawyer.

9.5   How soon does my spouse have to start paying support for the children?

Your spouse may begin paying you support voluntarily at any time. A temporary order for support will give you the right to collect the support if your spouse stops paying. Talk to your lawyer about court hearings for temporary support in your county. It is possible that the judge will not order child support to start until the first of the following month.

9.6   How is the amount of child support I'll receive or pay figured?

The *Florida Child Support Guidelines* were created to establish the standards by which your child support is calculated. According to the guidelines, both parents have a duty to contribute to the support of their children in proportion to their respective net incomes. As a result, both your income and the income of your spouse will factor into the child support calculation.

Both you and your spouse will be required to complete a financial affidavit and provide supporting documents clarifying your income. Supporting documents could include pay stubs, tax returns, bank statements, support orders for other children, and benefits information.

Child support that is higher or lower than what the guidelines provide for may be awarded in certain cases, for example:

- Extraordinary medical, dental, or psychological needs
- When a child is disabled with special needs
- Seasonal variations in income
- The age of the children

- Whenever the application of the guidelines in an individual case would be unjust or inappropriate.

When a judge orders an amount of support that is different from the guideline amount, it is referred to as a *deviation.*

Due to the complexity of calculations under the guidelines, many attorneys use computer software to calculate child support.

9.7 Will the type of custody arrangement or the amount of parenting time I have impact the amount of child support I receive?

It can. The child support guidelines allow provide for a calculation that can be adjusted based upon "substantial time-sharing". For this reason, it is essential that you discuss child support with your attorney prior to reaching any agreements with your spouse regarding parenting time.

9.8 Is overtime pay considered in the calculation of child support?

Yes, if your overtime is a regular part of your employment and you can actually expect to earn regularly. The judge can consider your work history, the degree of control you have over your overtime, and the nature of the field in which you work.

9.9 Will rental income be factored into my child support, or just my salary?

Yes. Income from other sources may be considered in determining the amount of child support.

9.10 My spouse has a college degree, but refuses to get a job. Will the court consider this in determining the amount of child support?

The earning capacity of your spouse may be considered instead of current income. The court can look at your spouse's work history, education, skills, health, and job opportunities.

If you believe your spouse is earning substantially less than the income she or he is capable of earning, provide your attorney with details. Ask about making a case for child support based on earning capacity instead of actual income.

9.11 One the final order is entered, will I get the child support directly from my spouse or from the state?

Florida law requires that an order for child support be withheld from the income of the payor of child support, unless there is a good reason not to have the support automatically withheld. This is a change from years past, when only those who were behind in their child support had it taken from their wages. Today, employers routinely withhold child support from employee wages just as they withhold taxes or retirement.

If the parent's income is not being withheld by his or her employer, the parent would either make the payments directly to the other parent, the clerk of court, or the Florida State Disbursement Center. Payments can be made either electronically or by mail. The clerk or disbursement center then sends the child support to the parent receiving support.

9.12 If my spouse sends in a child support payment to the state, how quickly will the state mail me a check?

A number of factors which affect how quickly your child support payment will be paid to you after it is received by the disbursement center, such as whether it is an out-of-state check or a certified check.

The disbursement center can mail you your child support check or you may decide to receive your child support by direct deposit or debit card. It may take three to five business days for processing through the mail. More information can be found on the Florida Department of Revenue Child Support Services website www.dor.myflorida.com. You can also check the status of payments at www.childsupport.state.fl.us.

9.13 Is there any reason not to pay or receive payments directly to or from my spouse once the court has entered a child support order?

Yes. Once a child support order is entered by the court, the Florida Department of Revenue Child Support Payment Center keeps a record of all support paid. If the payment is not made through the center, the state's records will show that you are behind in your child support.

Direct payments of child support can also result in misunderstandings between parents. The payor may have intended the money to pay a child support payment, but the parent receiving the support may have thought it was extra money to help with the child's expenses.

The payment of support through the payment center protects both parents. If a direct payment is made, be sure a notarized receipt is signed and filed with the clerk of court of the county in which your child support order was entered. This is important so that the state's records remain accurate. If no receipt is filed for a direct payment, it may later be considered a gift.

9.14　Can I go to the courthouse to pick up my child support payment?

No. The clerk of court will not give you the payment directly. They will require a mailing address.

9.15　How soon can I expect my child support payments to start arriving once the final order is entered?

A number of factors may affect the date on which you will begin receiving your child support. Here are the usual steps in the process:

- A child support amount and start date for the support is decided either by agreement between you and your spouse or by the judge.
- Either your attorney or your spouse's attorney for prepares the court order and the income deduction order.
- The attorney who did not write the court order and income deduction order reviews and approves them.
- The court order and income deduction orders are taken to the judge for signature.
- The clerk of court or the Florida State Disbursement Unit will establish and account once they receive the orders.
- Your spouse's employer withholds the support from the paycheck.
- The child support is transferred by the employer into the State Disbursement Unit payment center.
- The payment center sends the money to you, either by direct deposit or mail.

As you can see, there are a lot of steps in this process. Plan your budget knowing that the initial payment of child support might be delayed.

9.16 Will some amount of child support be withheld from every paycheck?

It depends upon the employer's policy and how you are paid. If support is due on the first of the month, the employer has the full month to withhold the amount ordered to be paid. If an employer issues paychecks twice a month, it is possible that half of the support will be withheld from each check and paid in to the Florida State Disbursement Payment Center at the end of the month.

If an employer issues checks every other week, which is twenty-six pay periods per year, there will be some months in which a third paycheck is issued. Consequently, it is possible that no child support will be withheld from the wages paid in that third check of the month, or that some checks will be for less than 50 percent of the monthly amount due.

Example: Suppose child support is $650 per month. Payor is paid every other Friday, or twenty-six times per year. The employer may withhold $300 per pay check for child support. While most months the support received will be $600, for a few months it will be $900. By the end of the year, however, the payor will have paid the same amount as if $650 had been paid each month.

Over time, child support payments typically fall into a routine schedule which makes it easier for both the payor and the recipient of support to plan their budgets.

9.17 If my spouse has income other than from an employer, is it still possible to get a court order to withhold my child support from his income?

Yes. Child support can be automatically withheld from a most sources of income. These may include unemployment, worker's compensation, retirement plans, and investment income.

9.18 The person I am divorcing is not the biological parent of my child. Can I still collect child support from my spouse?

Perhaps. Your spouse may be ordered to pay child support under certain circumstances. Among the factors the court will consider is whether your spouse is acting in the role of a parent to your child.

Discuss the facts of your case with your lawyer in detail. When you are clear about what will be in the best interest of your child, your attorney can support you in developing a strategy for your case which takes into consideration not only child support but also the future relationship of your spouse with your child.

9.19 Can I collect child support from both the biological parent and the adoptive parent of my child?

When your child was adopted, the biological parent's duty to support your child ended. However, it may be possible for you to collect past due child support from the period of time before the adoption.

9.20 What happens with child support when our children go to other parent's home for summer vacation? Is child support still due?

It depends. Whether child support is adjusted during extended parenting times with the noncustodial parent depends upon the court order in your case.

Before your divorce decree is entered by the court, talk with your lawyer about child support adjustments if you are anticipating that the parent paying support is will have the child for an extended period.

9.21 What is a *child support hearing officer?*

Although it is likely that your child support will be decided by the judge hearing your divorce, *child support hearing officers* are also authorized to hear matters regarding child support and spousal support. Hearing officers are attorneys who are appointed to conduct hearings in the same manner as a judge.

After hearing the evidence, the hearing officer will draw conclusions regarding the facts and make recommendations to the judge. The judge then has the authority to enter an order based upon the hearing officer's written report.

If you are dissatisfied with the hearing officer's findings and recommendations, talk to your attorney right away about filing an objection.

9.22 After the divorce, if I choose to live with my new partner rather than marry, can I still collect child support?

Yes. Although spousal support (alimony) may end if you live with your partner, child support does not terminate for this reason.

9.23 Can I still collect child support if I move to another state?

Yes. A move out of state will not end your right to receive child support. However, the amount of child support could be changed if other circumstances change, such as income or costs for exercising parenting time.

9.24 Can I expect to continue to receive child support if I remarry?

Yes. Your child support will continue even if you remarry.

9.25 How long can I expect to receive child support? What if I have a disabled child?

Under Florida law, child support is ordinarily ordered to be paid until the child dies, marries, is emancipated (becomes self-supporting), or reaches the age of nineteen.

If you have a child that was disabled before his/her eighteenth birthday, you may be entitled to receive support as that child becomes an adult. Make sure you have appropriate documentation detailing the child's disability.

9.26 Does interest accrue on past-due child support?

Yes, interest accrues on past-due child support. The interest rate should be set forth in your decree based upon the interest rate in effect under state law on the date your decree is entered.

9.27 What can I do if my former spouse refuses to pay child support?

If your former spouse is not paying child support, you may take action to enforce the court order either with the help of your lawyer or the assistance of the Department of Revenue Child Support Office attorney. Unlike a private attorney, you do not pay for the services of the Department of Revenue.

Visit the website for the Florida Department of Revenue Child Support services at www. dor.myflorida.com to apply for services online or for the local office.

The judge may order payment of both the current amount of support and an additional amount to be paid each month until the past due child support (referred to as *arrearages*) is paid in full.

You may request that your former spouse's federal tax refunds be sent directly to the Florida State Disbursement Center. It may also be possible to garnish a checking or savings account.

Driver's licenses may also be suspended if a parent falls behind in child support payments. However, if there is a payment plan for the payment of arrearages, then licenses will not be suspended.

Your former spouse may also be found in contempt of court if the failure to pay support is intentional. Possible consequences include being fined or jailed.

To review, if you are not receiving child support, you have these options:

- Call your attorney
- Call The Department of Revenue Child Support help number at (800) 622-KIDS (5437)
- Visit the Department of Revenue website at www.dor. myflorida.com
- Visit your local Department of Revenue child support office.

9.28 At what point will the state help me collect back-child support, and what methods do they use?

It depends. When the state will help you collect back child support and the methods they will use can depend upon the amount of back child support owed.

Driver's, recreational, and professional licenses can be suspended, federal income tax refunds can be intercepted and, where more than $2,500 is owed, a passport hold may be sent to the passport office. In some cases, failure to pay child support can result in a jail sentence.

You must initiate contact with your attorney or the state if you want help in collecting your child support.

9.29 I live outside of Florida. Will the money I spend on airline tickets to see my children impact my child support?

It might. If you expect to spend large sums of money for transportation in order to have parenting time with your children, talk to your attorney about how this might be taken into consideration when determining the amount of child support.

9.30 After the divorce, can my former spouse substitute buying sprees with the child for child support payments?

No. Purchases of gifts and clothing for a child do not relieve your former spouse from an obligation to pay you child support.

9.31 Are expenses such as child care supposed to be taken out of my child support?

No. Child-care expenses are separate from child support because the *Florida Child Support Guidelines* recognize that child care for young children is often a tremendous expense. Therefore, the guidelines provide that each parent pay a percentage of the work or school related day care expenses in addition to the child support.

Other expenses for your child such as clothing, school lunches, and the cost for activities are ordinarily paid for by you if you are receiving child support according to the guidelines, unless the court order in your case provides otherwise.

9.32 Can my spouse be required by the decree to pay for our child's private elementary and high school education?

While the *Florida Child Support Guidelines* make no specific provision for private education tuition, some parents agree to include a provision in the decree for payment of such tuition because both of them believe it is important for their child.

If you want your spouse to share this expense for your child, talk it over with your lawyer. Be sure to provide your attorney with information regarding tuition, fees, and other expenses related to private education.

9.33 Can my spouse be required by the decree to contribute financially to our child's college education?

The legal duty of a parent to support a child does not include payment for college education. However, if your spouse agrees to pay this expense, it can be included in the final decree and it will be an enforceable court order. Such a provision is ordinarily included in a divorce decree only as a result of a negotiated settlement.

If your decree includes a provision for payment of college education expenses, be sure it is specific. Terms to consider include:

- What expenses are included? For example, tuition, room and board, books, fees, travel, etc.
- Is there a limit? For example, up to the level of the cost of attendance at one of the state universities or a certain dollar amount.
- When is payment due?
- For what period of time does it continue?
- Are there any limits on the type of education that will be paid for?

The greater the clarity in such a provision, the lower the risk is for misunderstanding or conflict years later.

10

Alimony

The mere mention of the word *alimony* might stir your emotions and start your stomach churning. If your spouse filed for divorce and sought alimony, you might see it as is a double injustice—your marriage is ending and you feel like you have to pay for it, too. If you are seeking spousal support, you might feel hurt and confused that your spouse is resistant to helping to support you, even though you interrupted your career to stay home and care for your children.

Learning more about Florida's laws on alimony, also referred to as spousal support, can help you move from your emotional reaction to it to the reality of possible outcomes in your case. Uncertainty about the precise amount of alimony that may be awarded or the number of years it might be paid is not unusual. Work closely with your lawyer. Be open to possibilities. Try looking at it from your spouse's perspective.

With the help of your lawyer, you will know the best course of action to take toward an alimony decision you can live with after your divorce is over.

10.1   Which gets calculated first, child support or alimony?

Alimony. Child support is determined from the income which is available after the amount of alimony is determined.

10.2   What's the difference between *spousal support* and *alimony?*

In Florida, *alimony* and *spousal support* have the same meaning.

10.3   Are their different types of alimony?

In Florida, there are several types of alimony—temporary, rehabilitative, periodic, permanent, and lump sum.

If the court awards alimony while that divorce is pending, it is generally called *temporary alimony*. The purpose of temporary support is to maintain the status quo of the finances while the divorce is pending. Keep in mind that an award of temporary support does not guarantee an award of alimony once the dissolution is over.

After the dissolution, some judges may award alimony for a fixed period of time or consider a *rehabilitative* plan to enable you to or your spouse to obtain further training or education to be more fully self-supporting.

Permanent alimony is permanent, however, there are instances when the judge would consider modifying or eliminating, for example, if you or your spouse remarry, live in a supportive relationship, or the financial circumstances of either of you substantially and permanent changes.

Lump sum alimony is a fixed amount of money that can be ordered to be paid at one time or over a period of time. Lump sum alimony is not subject to modification or elimination.

10.4   How will I know if I am eligible to receive alimony?

Talk with your attorney about whether you are a candidate for alimony. The opinions of Florida judges about awarding alimony can vary greatly. Among the factors that may affect your eligibility to receive alimony are:

- The length of your marriage
- Your contributions to the marriage, including the interruption of your career for the care of children or to support your spouse's career
- Your education, work history, health, income, and earning capacity
- Your overall financial situation compared to that of your spouse
- Your need for support
- Your spouse's ability to pay support

Every case for alimony is unique. Providing your lawyer with clear and detailed information about the facts of your marriage and current situation will increase the likelihood of a fair outcome for you.

10.5   What information should I provide to my attorney if I want alimony?

If your attorney advises you that you may be a candidate for alimony, be sure to provide complete facts about your situation, including:

- A history of the interruptions in your education or career for the benefit of your spouse, including transfers or moves due to your spouse's employment
- A history of the interruptions in your education or career for raising children, including periods during which you worked part-time
- Your complete educational background, including the dates of your schooling or training and degrees earned
- Your work history, including the names of your employers, the dates of your employment, your duties, your pay, and the reason you left
- Any pensions or other benefits lost due to the interruption of your career for the benefit of the marriage
- Your health history, including any current diagnoses, treatments, limitations, and medications
- Your monthly living expenses, including anticipated future expenses such as health insurance and tax on alimony
- A complete list of the debts for you and your spouse
- Income for you and your spouse, including all sources

Also include any other facts that might support your need for alimony, such as other contributions you made to the marriage, upcoming medical treatment, or a lack of jobs in the field in which you were formerly employed.

No two alimony cases are alike. The better the information your lawyer has about your situation, the easier it will be for him or her to assess your case for alimony.

10.6 **My spouse told me that because I had an affair during the marriage, I have no chance to get alimony even though I quit my job and have cared for our children for many years. Is it true that I have no case?**

Your right to alimony will be based upon many factors, but having an affair is not an absolute bar to getting spousal support.

10.7 **How is the amount of alimony calculated?**

Unlike child support, there are not specific guidelines for determining the amount of alimony. A judge will look at the expenses and incomes of you and your spouse, after considering whether you are entitled to alimony.

Judges are given a lot of discretion to make their own decision on alimony without the benefit of specific guidelines. Consequently, the outcome of an alimony ruling by a judge can be one of the most unpredictable aspects of your divorce.

10.8 **My spouse makes a lot more money than he reports on our tax return, but he hides it. How can I prove my spouse's real income to show he can afford to pay alimony?**

Alert your attorney to your concerns. Your lawyer can then take a number of actions to determine your spouse's income with greater accuracy. This is likely to include:

- More thorough discovery
- An examination of check registers and bank deposits
- Reviewing purchases made in cash
- Inquiring about travel
- Depositions of third parties who have knowledge of income or spending by your spouse
- Subpoena of records of places where your spouse has made large purchases or received income
- Comparing income claimed with expenses paid

By partnering with your lawyer, you may be able to build a case to establish your spouse's actual income as greater than is shown on your tax returns. If you filed joint tax returns, discuss with your lawyer any other implications on those returns of erroneous information.

10.9 I want to be sure the records on the alimony I pay are accurate, especially for tax purposes. What's the best way to ensure this?

If you are paying the alimony and child support directly to your spouse, you can give two separate checks and designate in the memo line whether the payment is alimony or child support.

If you are paying alimony and child support and you are order to make the payments to the Florida State Disbursement Unit, although they will maintain the designation of payments, it is still important to keep your own records of the payments.

If you pay alimony but no child support, ask the court to order the payments to be made through the clerk of court in the county where the order is entered.

By avoiding direct payments to your former spouse, you and he or she will have accurate records. To avoid an audit by the Internal Revenue Service, you must deduct the same amount of alimony that your spouse is reporting as income on your tax returns.

10.10 How is the purpose of alimony different from the payment of my property settlement?

Spousal support and the division of property serve two distinct purposes. The purpose of alimony is to pay for your continued support, whereas the purpose of a property division is to distribute the marital assets fairly and equitably between you and your spouse.

10.11 How long can I expect to receive alimony?

The trend in Florida has been away from lifetime alimony awards. Like your right to receive alimony, how long you will receive alimony will depend upon the facts of your case and the judge's philosophy toward alimony. In general, the longer your marriage, the stronger your case is for a long-term alimony award.

You may receive only temporary alimony, or you may receive alimony for several years. Talk to your attorney about the facts of your case to get a clearer picture of the possible outcomes in your situation. Unless you and your spouse agree otherwise, your alimony will terminate upon your remarriage or the death of either of you.

10.12 If I live with someone or get remarried does that affect my alimony?

If you live with a partner, the court can terminate your alimony if the court determines that you are in a supportive relations. Under Florida law, your alimony ends upon remarriage.

10.13 Can I continue to collect alimony if I move to a different state?

Yes. The duty of your former spouse to follow a court order to pay alimony does not end simply because you move to another state, unless this is a specific provision in your decree.

10.14 What can I do if my spouse stops paying alimony?

If your spouse stops paying alimony, see your attorney about your options for enforcing your court order. The judge may order the support taken from a source of your spouse's income or from a financial account belonging to your spouse.

If your spouse is intentionally refusing to pay spousal support, talk to your attorney about whether pursuing a contempt of court action would be effective. In a contempt action, your spouse may be ordered to appear in court and provide evidence explaining why support has not been paid. Possible consequences for contempt of court include a jail sentence or a fine.

10.15 Can I return to court to modify alimony?

It depends. If your divorce decree provides that your alimony order is "non-modifiable," then you may not have it modified. Also, if no award of alimony was made in the decree, you will not be entitled to receive alimony in the future.

If there has been a material change in the circumstances of either you or your spouse, you may seek to have alimony modified. Examples include a serious illness or the loss of or obtaining of a job.

A petition to modify alimony for the purposes of seeking additional alimony may not be filed if the time for payment of alimony allowed under your original decree has already passed.

If you think you have a basis to modify your alimony, contact your attorney at once to be sure a timely modification request is filed with the court.

11

Division of Property

You never imagined you would face losing the house you and your spouse worked so hard for and made into a home where you raised your children and celebrated family traditions. Now, your spouse wants it and your attorney says it might have to be sold.

During the divorce, you will have to decide whether you or your spouse will take ownership of everything from bathroom towels to the stock portfolios. Suddenly you find yourself have a strong attachment to the lamp in the living room and the holiday ornaments in the garage. Why do the cookie jars now have such a sentimental value?

It is best for your and your spouse to come to a resolution regarding the division personal and household items. Work with your attorney to determine whether property such as a family business or real estate should be valued by an expert. There are many factors to consider when deciding whether to keep property, giving it to your spouse, or having it sold. From tax consequences to replacement value, your attorney can help you evaluate these decisions.

Like all aspects of your divorce, consider all the options carefully. By starting with the items that can easily divided between you and your spouse, you can avoid paying attorney to litigate the value of items they may be valued less than your attorney's hourly rate.

11.1   What system does Florida use for dividing property?

Florida law provides for an equitable division of the property and debts acquired during your marriage. There is a presumption that the division of property shall be equal. The court will consider several factors that would not justify an equal division of the property including the following:

- The contributions of each spouse during the marriage, including one spouse's raising the children
- The financial resources of each spouse
- One spouse's sacrifices in the other spouse's career building
- Maintaining the marital home for raising any minor children
- The benefit of maintaining an asset like a business or other income producing asset

11.2   What does *community property* mean?

Community property is a term used in several states which have a community-property system for dividing assets in a divorce. Florida is not a community property state. In states having community property laws, each spouse holds a one-half interest in most property acquired.

11.3   How is it determined who gets the house?

If you and your spouse are unable to reach agreement regarding the house, the judge will decide who keeps it or whether it will be sold.

11.4   Should I sell the house during the divorce proceedings?

As a general rule, you cannot sell your home during the divorce proceedings unless both you and your spouse have agreed to do so or there is a court order allowing you to do so. Selling your home is a big decision. To help you decide what is right for you, ask yourself these questions:

- What will be the impact on my children if the home is sold?
- Can I afford to stay in the house after the divorce?

- After the divorce, will I be willing to give the house and yard the time, money, and physical energy required for its maintenance?
- Is it necessary for me to sell the house to pay a share of the equity to my spouse, or are there other options?
- Would my life be easier if I were in a smaller or simpler home?
- Would I prefer to move closer to the support of friends and family?
- What is the state of the housing market in my community?
- What are the benefits of remaining in this home?
- Can I retain the existing mortgage or will I have to refinance?
- Will I have a higher or lower interest rate if I sell the house?
- Can I see myself living in a different home?
- Will I have the means to acquire another home?
- If I don't retain the home and my spouse asks for it, what affect will this have on my custody case?
- Will my spouse agree to the sale of the house?
- What will be the real estate commission?
- What will be the costs of preparing the house for sale?

Selling a home is more than just a legal or financial decision. Consider what is important to you in creating your life after divorce when deciding whether to sell your home.

11.5   What is meant by *equity* in my home?

Regardless of who is awarded your house, the court will consider whether the spouse not receiving the house should be compensated for the equity in the house. By *equity* we mean the difference between the value of the home and the amount owed in mortgages against the property.

For example, if the first mortgage is $50,000 and the second mortgage from a home equity loan is $10,000, the total debt owed against the house is $60,000. If your home is valued at $100,000, the equity in your home is $40,000. (The $100,000 value less the $60,000 in mortgages equals $40,000 in equity).

If one of the parties remains in the home, the issue of how to give the other party his or her share of the equity must be considered.

11.6   How will the equity in our house be divided?

If your home is going to be sold, the equity in the home will most likely be divided at the time of the sale, after the costs of the sale have been paid.

If either you or your spouse will be awarded the house, there are a number of options for the other party being compensated for his or her share of the equity in the marital home. These could include:

- The spouse who does not receive the house receives other assets (for example, retirement funds) to compensate for the value of the equity.
- The person who remains in the home agrees to refinance the home at some future date and to pay the other party his or her share of the equity.
- The parties agree that the property be sold at a future date, or upon the happening of a certain event such as the youngest child completing high school or the remarriage of the party keeping the home.

As the residence is often among the most valuable assets considered in a divorce, it is important that you and your attorney discuss the details of its disposition. These include:

- Valuation of the property
- Refinancing to remove a party from liability for the mortgage
- The dates on which certain actions should be taken, such as listing the home for sale
- The real estate agent
- Costs of preparing the home for sale
- Making mortgage payments

If you and your spouse do not agree regarding which of you will remain in the home, the court will decide who keeps it or may order the property sold.

11.7 Who keeps all the household goods until the decree is signed?

The court will ordinarily not make any decisions about who keeps the household goods on a temporary basis. Most couples attempt to resolve these issues on their own rather than incur legal fees to dispute household goods on a temporary basis.

11.8 How are assets such as cars, boats, and furniture divided, and when does this happen?

In most cases spouses are able to reach their own agreements about how to divide personal property, such as household furnishings and vehicles.

If you and your spouse disagree about how to divide certain items, it can be wise to consider which are truly valuable to you, financially or otherwise. Perhaps some of them can be easily replaced. Always look to see whether it is a good use of your attorney fees to argue over items of personal property. If a negotiated settlement cannot be reached, the issue of the division of your property will be made by the judge at trial.

11.9 What is meant by a *property inventory* and how detailed should mine be?

A *property inventory* is a listing of the property you own. It may also include a brief description of the property. Discuss with your attorney the level of inventory detail needed to benefit your case.

Factors to consider when creating your inventory may include:

- The extent to which you anticipate you and your spouse will disagree regarding the division of your property
- Whether you anticipate a dispute regarding the value of the property either you or your spouse is retaining
- Whether you will have continued access to the property if a later inventory is needed or whether your spouse will retain control of the property
- Whether you and your spouse are likely to disagree about which items are premarital, inherited, or gifts from someone other than your spouse

In addition to creating an inventory, your attorney may request that you prepare a list of the property that you and your spouse have already divided or a list of the items you want but your spouse has not agreed to give to you.

If you do not have continued access to your property, talk to your attorney about taking photographs or obtaining access to the property to complete your inventory.

11.10 How and when are liquid assets like bank accounts and stocks divided?

Talk with your attorney early in your case about the benefits of a temporary restraining order to reduce the risk that your spouse will transfer money out of financial accounts or transfer other assets.

In many cases couples will agree to divide bank accounts equally at the outset of the case. However, this may not be advisable in your case. Discuss with your attorney whether you should keep an accounting of how you spend money used from a bank account while your divorce is in progress.

Stocks are ordinarily a part of the final agreement for the division of property and debts. If you and your spouse cannot agree on how your investments should be divided, the judge will make the decision at trial.

11.11 How is pet custody determined?

Under Florida law, pets are considered personal property and, therefore, the courts will not consider a "custody" arrangement and "visitation" with the pet. If it is important to you to be awarded one of your family pets, discuss the matter with your attorney.

11.12 How will our property in another state be divided?

For the purposes of dividing your assets, out-of-state property is treated the same as property in Florida. Although a Florida court cannot order a change in the title to property located in another state, a judge can order your spouse either to turn the property over to you or to sign a deed or other document to transfer title to you.

11.13 I worked like a dog for years to support my family while my spouse completed an advanced degree. Do I have a right to any of my spouse's future earnings?

Your contributions during the marriage are a factor to be considered in both the division of the property and debts, as well as any award of alimony. Be sure to give your attorney a complete history of your contributions to the marriage and ask about their impact on the outcome of your case.

11.14 Are all of the assets—such as property, bank accounts and inheritances—that I had prior to my marriage still going to be mine after the divorce?

It depends. In many cases the court will allow a party to retain an asset brought into the marriage called *premarital assets,* but the following are questions the court will consider in making its determination:

- Can the premarital asset be clearly traced? For example, if you continue to own a vehicle that you brought into the marriage, it is likely that it will be awarded to you. However, if you brought a vehicle into the marriage, sold it during the marriage, and spent the proceeds, it is less likely that the court will consider awarding you its value

- Did you keep the property separate and titled in your name, or did you comingle it with marital assets? Premarital assets you kept separate may be more likely to be awarded to you.

- Did the other spouse contribute to the increase in the value of the premarital asset, and can the value of that increase be proven? For example, suppose a woman owned a home prior to her marriage. After the marriage, the parties live in the home, continuing to make mortgage payments and improvements to the home. At the time of the divorce, the husband seeks a portion of the equity in the home. The court might consider the value of the home at the time of the marriage, any contributions to the increase in equity made by the husband, and the evidence of the value of those contributions.

11.15   Will I get to keep my engagement ring?

If your engagement ring was given to you prior to your marriage, it will be considered a gift and treated as premarital property that you can keep.

11.16   Can I keep gifts and inheritances I received during the marriage?

Similar rules apply to gifts and inheritances received during the marriage as apply to premarital assets, that is, assets you owned prior to the marriage and are generally referred to as nonmarital assets.

Gifts that you and your spouse gave to one another may be treated as any other marital asset. For gifts received during the marriage, such as a gift from a parent, the court will need to determine whether the gift was made to one party or to both. Inheritances are generally nonmarital assets, however, if they are comingled, meaning put into joint accounts it is more difficult to establish them as nonmarital. Whether you will be entitled to keep assets you inherited, assuming they are still in existence, will depend upon the unique circumstances of your case. When dividing the marital estate, the court may consider the fact that one spouse is allowed to keep substantial nonmarital assets such as an inheritance.

The following factors increase the probability that you will be entitled to keep your inheritance:

- It has been kept separate from the marital assets, such as in a separate account.
- It is titled in your name only.
- It can be clearly identified.
- It has not been commingled with marital assets.
- Your spouse has not contributed to its care, operation, or improvement.

It is less likely that you will be awarded your full inheritance if:

- It was commingled with marital assets.
- Its origin cannot be traced.
- You have placed your spouse's name on the title.
- Your spouse has contributed to the increase in the value of the inheritance.

If keeping your inheritance is important to you, talk to your attorney about the information needed to build your case.

11.17 If my spouse and I can't decide who gets what, who decides? Can that person's decision be contested?

If you and your spouse cannot agree on the division of your property, the judge will make the determination after considering the evidence at your trial.

If either party is dissatisfied with the decision reached by the judge, an appeal to a higher court is possible.

11.18 What is a *property settlement agreement?*

A *property settlement agreement* is a written document that includes all of the financial agreements you and your spouse have reached in your divorce. This may include the division of property, debts, child support, alimony, insurance, and attorney fees.

The property settlement may be a separate document, or it may be incorporated into the decree of dissolution, which is the final court order dissolving your marriage.

11.19 How are the values of property determined?

The value of some assets like bank accounts, are usually not disputed. The value of other assets, such as homes or personal property, are more likely to be disputed.

If your case proceeds to trial, you may give your opinion of the value of property you own. You or your spouse may also have certain property appraised by an expert. In such cases it may be necessary to have the appraiser appear at trial to give testimony regarding the appraisal and the value of the asset.

If you own substantial assets for which the value is likely to be disputed, talk to your attorney early in your case about the benefits and costs of expert witnesses.

11.20 What does *date of valuation* mean?

Because the value of assets can go up or down while a divorce is pending, it can be necessary to determine a set date for valuing the marital assets. This is referred to as the *date of valuation*. You and your spouse can agree on the date the assets should be valued. If you cannot agree, the judge will decide the date of valuation.

Among the most common dates used are the date of separation, the date of the filing of the divorce complaint, or the date of the divorce trial.

11.21 What happens after my spouse and I approve the property settlement agreement? Do we still have to go to court?

After you and your spouse sign your name to approve the property settlement agreement or decree, it must still be approved by your judge at a final hearing. A final hearing can be scheduled after the passing of the twenty-one-day mandatory waiting period under Florida law, assuming you and your spouse have also resolved all matters pertaining to your minor children.

If a property settlement agreement is reached by the parties, a court date for your final hearing can often be obtained earlier than a trial date, because a final hearing requires much less time than a trial.

11.22 If my spouse and I think our property settlement agreement is fair, why does the judge have to approve it?

The judge has a duty to ensure that all property settlement agreements in divorces are fair and reasonable. For this reason, your judge must review your agreement. The judge can consider the facts and circumstances of your case when reviewing the agreement. Not every case will result in an equal division of the assets and debts from the marriage, although this is very common.

11.23 What happens to our individual checking and savings accounts during and after the divorce?

Regardless of whose name is on the account, bank accounts may be considered marital assets and may be divided by the court.

Discuss with your attorney the benefits of a temporary restraining order to protect bank accounts, how to use these accounts while the case is pending, and the date on which financial accounts should be valued.

11.24 Who gets the interest from certificates of deposit, dividends from stock holdings during the divorce proceedings?

Whether you or your spouse receives interest from these assets is decided as a part of the overall division of your property and debts.

11.25 Do each one of our financial accounts have to be divided in half if we agree to an equal division of our assets?

No. Rather than incurring the administrative challenges and expense of dividing each asset in half, you and your spouse can decide that one of you will take certain assets equal to the value of assets taken by the spouse. If necessary, one of you can agree to make a cash payment to the other to make an equitable division.

11.26 What factors determine whether I can get at least half of my spouse's business?

Many factors determine whether you will get a share of your spouse's business and in what form you might receive it. Among the factors the court will look at are:

- Whether your spouse owned the business prior to your marriage
- Your role, if any, in operating the business or increasing its value
- The overall division of the property and debts

If you or your spouse own a business, it is important that you work with your attorney early in your case to develop a strategy for valuing the business and making your case for how it should be treated in the division of property and debts.

11.27 My spouse and I have owned and run our own business together for many years. Can I be forced out of it?

Deciding what should happen with a family business when divorce occurs can be a challenge. Because of the risk for future conflict between you and your spouse, the value of the business is likely to be substantially decreased if you both remain owners.

In discussing your options with your lawyer, consider the following questions:

- If one spouse retains ownership of the business, are there enough other assets for the other spouse to receive a fair share of the total marital assets?
- Which spouse has the skills and experience to continue running the business?
- What would you do if you weren't working in the business?
- What is the value of the business?
- What is the market for the business if it were to be sold?
- Could you remain an employee of the business for some period of time even if you were not an owner?

You and your spouse know your business best. With the help of your lawyers, you may be able to create a settlement that can satisfy you both. If not, the judge will make the decision for you at trial.

11.28 I suspect my spouse is hiding assets, but I can't prove it. How can I protect myself if I discover later that I was right?

Ask your lawyer to include language in your divorce decree to address your concern. Insist that it include an acknowledgment by your spouse that the agreement was based upon a full and complete disclosure of your spouse's financial situation. Discuss with your lawyer a provision that allows for setting aside the agreement if it is later discovered that assets were hidden.

11.29 My spouse says I'm not entitled to a share of his stock options because he gets to keep them only if he stays employed with his company. What are my rights?

Stock options are often a very valuable asset. They are also one of the most complex issues when dividing assets during a divorce fore these, among other reasons:

- Each company has its own rules about awarding and exercising stock options
- Complete information is needed from the employer
- There are different methods for calculating the value of stock options
- The reasons the options were given can impact the valuation, for example, some are given for future performance
- There is a cost and tax considerations when options are exercised

Rather than being awarded a portion of the stock options themselves, you are likely to receive a share of the proceeds when the stock options are exercised.

If either you or your spouse owns stock options, begin discussing this asset with your attorney early in your case to allow sufficient time to settle the issues or to be well prepared for trial.

11.30 What is a *prenuptial agreement* and how might it affect the property settlement phase of the divorce?

A *prenuptial agreement,* sometimes referred to as a *premarital agreement,* is a contract entered into between two people prior to their marriage. It can include provisions for how assets and debts will be divided in the event the marriage is terminated, as well as terms concerning child support or alimony.

Your property settlement is likely to be impacted by the terms of your prenuptial agreement if the agreement is upheld as valid by the court.

11.31 Can a prenuptial agreement be contested during the divorce?

Yes. The court may consider many factors in determining whether to uphold your prenuptial agreement. Among them are:

- Whether your agreement was entered into voluntarily
- Whether your agreement was fair and reasonable at the time it was signed

- Whether you and your spouse each gave a complete disclosure of your assets and debts
- Whether you and your spouse each had your own lawyer
- Whether you and your spouse each had enough time to consider the agreement

If your have a prenuptial agreement, bring a copy of it to the initial consultation with your attorney. Be sure to provide your lawyer with a detailed history of the facts and circumstances surrounding reaching and signing the agreement.

11.32 I've heard the old saying, "possession is nine-tenths of the law." Is that true during divorce proceedings?

It can be. Consulting with an attorney in before the filing of divorce can reduce the risk that assets will be hidden, transferred, or destroyed by your spouse. This is especially important if your spouse has a history of destroying property, incurring substantial debt, or transferring money without your knowledge.

These are among the possible actions you and your attorney can consider together include:

- Placing your family heirlooms or other valuables in a safe location
- Transferring some portion of financial accounts prior to filing for divorce
- Preparing an inventory of the personal property
- Taking photographs or a video of the property
- Obtaining copies of important financial records or statements
- Obtaining a restraining order before your spouse is served with notice of the divorce

Plans to leave the marital home should also be discussed in detail with your attorney, so that any actions taken early in your case are consistent with your ultimate goals.

Speak candidly with your lawyer about your concerns so that a plan can be developed which provides a level of protection that is appropriate to your circumstances.

11.33 I'm Jewish and want my husband to cooperate with obtaining a *get cooperation clause*, which is a divorce document under our religion. Can I get a court order for this?

Talk to your lawyer about obtaining a *get cooperation clause* in your divorce decree, including a provision regarding who should pay for it. At this time, the law regarding this has not been established in Florida.

11.34 Who will get the frozen embryo of my egg and my spouse's sperm that we have stored at the health clinic?

The law on this issue is still being established in Florida. The terms of your contract with the clinic may impact the rights you and your spouse may have to the embryo, so provide a copy of it to your attorney for review. If permissible under your contract, you and your spouse may want to consider donating the embryo to another couple.

11.35 Will debts be considered when determining the division of the property?

Yes. The court will consider the marital debts when dividing the property. For example, if you are awarded a car valued at $12,000, but you owe a $10,000 debt on the same vehicle, the court will take that debt into consideration in the overall division of the assets. Similarly, if one spouse agrees to pay substantial marital credit card debt, this obligation may also be considered in the final determination of the division of property and debts.

If your spouse incurred debts that you believe should be his or her sole responsibility, tell your attorney. Some debts may be considered nonmarital and treated separately from other debts incurred during the marriage. For example, if your spouse spent large sums of money on gambling or illegal drugs without your knowledge, you may be able to argue that those debts should be the sole responsibility of your spouse.

11.36 What happens to the property distribution if one of us dies before the divorce proceedings are completed?

If your spouse dies prior to your divorce decree being entered, you will be considered married and treated as a surviving spouse under the law. An exception to this may be if you and your spouse entered into a property settlement agreement.

12

Benefits: Insurance, Retirement, and Pensions

During your marriage, you might have taken certain employment benefits for granted. You might not have given much thought each month to having insurance through your spouse's work. When you find yourself in a divorce, suddenly these benefits come to the forefront of your mind.

You might also, even unconsciously, have seen your own employment retirement benefits as belonging to you and not your spouse, referring to "My 401(k)" or "My pension." After all, you are the one who went to work every day to earn it, right?

When you divorce, some benefits arising from your spouse's employment will end, some may continue for a period of time, and others may be divided between you. Retirement funds, in particular, are often one of the valuable marital assets to be divided in a divorce.

Whether the benefits are from your employer or your spouse's, with your attorney's help you will develop a better understanding of which benefits the law considers to be "yours" "mine," and "ours" for continuing or dividing.

12.1 Will my children continue to have health coverage through my spouse's work even though we're divorcing?

If either you or your spouse currently provides health insurance for your children, it is very likely that the court will order the insurance to remain in place for so long as it remains available and support is being paid for your child.

The cost of insurance for the children will be taken into consideration in determining the amount of child support to be paid.

12.2 Will I continue to have health insurance through my spouse's work after the divorce?

It depends. If your spouse currently provides health insurance for you, under the *Affordable Health Care Act,* also known as Obamacare, you may be treated as a spouse for health insurance purposes for the remainder of the calendar year following the entry of your divorce decree. However, some insurance companies refuse to treat a person as a spouse beyond thirty days after the entry of the divorce decree.

Investigate the cost of continuing on your spouse's employer-provided plans under a federal law known as *COBRA*. This coverage can be maintained for up to three years. However, the cost can be very high, so you will want to determine whether it's a realistic option.

Tell your attorney if you want to be kept on your spouse's health insurance policy for the remainder of the year. If you have no other health insurance, this is an important provision to be included in your divorce decree.

Begin early to investigate your options for your future health insurance. The cost of your health care is an important factor when pursuing spousal support and planning your post-divorce budget.

12.3 What is a QMCSO?

A *qualified medical child support order (QMCSO)* is a court order providing continued group health insurance coverage for a minor child. A QMCSO may also enable a parent to obtain other information about the plan, without having to go through the parent who has the coverage. Rather than allowing only the parent with the insurance to be reimbursed for a claim, under a QMSO, a health insurance plan is required to reimburse directly whoever actually paid the child's medical expense.

12.4 How many years must I have been married before I'm eligible to receive a part of my spouse's retirement fund or pension?

Even if you have not been married for a long time, you may be entitled to a portion of your spouse's retirement fund or pension accumulated during the marriage. For example, if you were married for three years and your spouse contributed $10,000 to a 401(k) plan during the marriage, it is possible that the court would award you half of the value of the contribution when dividing your property and debts.

12.5 I contributed to my pension plan for ten years before I got married. Will my spouse get half of my entire pension?

Probably not. It is more likely the court will award your spouse only a portion of your retirement that was acquired during the marriage.

If either you or your spouse made premarital contributions to a pension or retirement plan, be sure to let your attorney know. This is information essential to determine which portion of the retirement plan should be treated as premarital and thus unlikely to be shared.

12.6 I plan to keep my same job after my divorce, will my former spouse get half of the money I contribute to my retirement plan after my divorce?

No. Your former spouse should be entitled to a portion of your retirement accumulated only during the marriage. Talk with your attorney so that the language of the court order ensures protection of your postdivorce retirement contributions.

12.7 Am I still entitled to a share of my spouse's retirement even though I never contributed to one during our twenty-five-year marriage?

Probably. Retirements are often the most valuable asset accumulated during a marriage. Consequently, your judge will consider the retirement along with all of the other marital assets and debts when determining a fair division.

12.8   My lawyer says I'm entitled to a share of my spouse's retirement. How can I find out how much I get and when I'm eligible to receive it?

More than one factor will determine your rights to collect from your spouse's retirement. One factor will be the terms of the court order dividing the retirement. The court order will tell you whether you are entitled to a set dollar amount, a percentage, or a fraction to be determined based upon the length of your marriage and how long your spouse continues working.

Another factor will be the terms of the retirement plan itself. Some provide for lump sum withdrawals; others issue payments in monthly installments. Review both the terms of your court order and contact the plan administrator to obtain the clearest understanding of your rights and benefits.

12.9   If I am eligible to receive my spouse's retirement benefits, do I have to be sixty-five to collect them?

It depends upon the terms of your spouse's retirement plan. In some cases, it is possible to begin receiving your share at the earliest date your spouse is eligible to receive them, regardless of whether he or she elects to do so. Check the terms of your spouse's plan to learn your options.

12.10   What happens if my former spouse is old enough to receive benefits but I'm not?

Ordinarily you will be eligible to begin receiving your share of the benefits when your former spouse begins his or hers. Depending upon the plan, you may be eligible to receive them sooner.

12.11   Am I entitled to cost-of-living increases on my share of my spouse's retirement?

It depends. If your spouse has a retirement plan that includes a provision for a *cost-of-living allowance (COLA),* talk to your lawyer about whether this can be included in the court order dividing the retirement.

12.12 What circumstances might prevent my getting part of my spouse's retirement benefits?

Some government pension plans are not subject to division. If you or your spouse are employed by a government agency, talk with your lawyer about how this may affect the property settlement in your case.

12.13 Does the death of my spouse affect the payout of retirement benefits to me or to our children?

It depends upon both the nature of your spouse's retirement plan and the terms of the court order dividing the retirement. If you want to be eligible for survivorship benefits from your spouse's pension, discuss the issue with your attorney before your case is settled or goes to trial. He or she can advise you.

Some plans allow only a surviving spouse or former spouse to be a beneficiary. Others may allow for the naming of an alternate beneficiary, such as your children.

12.14 How can I be sure I'll get my share of my former spouse's retirement when I am entitled to it years from now?

Rather than relying upon your former spouse to pay you a share of a future retirement, your best protection is a court order that provides for the retirement or pension plan administrator to pay the money directly to you. This type of court order is often referred to as a *qualified domestic relations order (QDRO)* or, in the case of federal retirement plans, a *court order acceptable for processing (COAP)*. Such orders help ensure that a nonemployee spouse receives his or her share directly from the employee spouse's plan.

Obtaining a QDRO or COAP is a critical step in the divorce process. They can be complex documents, and a number of steps are required to reduce future concerns about enforcement and fully protect your rights. These court orders must comply with numerous technical rules and be approved by the plan administrator, which is often located outside of Florida.

Whenever possible, court orders dividing retirement plans should be entered at the same time as the decree of dissolution.

12.15 If my former spouse passes on before I do, can I still collect his or her Social Security benefits?

It depends. If you were married to your spouse for ten or more years and you have not remarried, you may be eligible for benefits. Contact your local Social Security Administration office or visit the SSA website at www.ssa.gov.

12.16 What orders might the court enter regarding life insurance?

The judge may order you or your spouse to maintain a life insurance policy to ensure that future support payments are made. In most cases you will be required to pay for your own life insurance after your divorce, and you should include this as an expense in your monthly budget.

12.17 Because we share children, should I consider my spouse as a beneficiary on my life insurance?

It depends upon your intentions. If your intention is to give the money to your former spouse, by all means name the other parent as beneficiary.

However, if you intend the life insurance proceeds to be used for the benefit of your children, talk with your attorney about your options. You may consider naming a trustee to manage the life insurance proceeds on behalf of your children, and there may be reasons to choose someone other than your former spouse.

12.18 Can the court require in the decree that I be the beneficiary of my spouse's insurance policy, so long as the children are minors or indefinitely?

When a court order is entered for life insurance, it is ordinarily for the purposes of ensuring payment of future support and will terminate when the support obligation has ended.

12.19 My spouse is in the military. What are my rights to benefits after the divorce?

As the former spouse of a military member, the types of benefits to which you may be entitled are typically determined by the number of years you were married, the number of years yours spouse was in the military while you were married, and whether or not you have remarried. Be sure you obtain accurate information about these dates.

Among the benefits you may be eligible are:

- A portion of your spouse's military retirement pay
- A survivor benefit in the event of your spouse's death
- Health care or participation in a temporary, transitional health-care program
- Use of certain military facilities, such as the commissary

While your divorce is pending, educate yourself about your right to future military benefits so that you can plan for your future with clarity. If your divorce is still pending, contact your base legal office, or for more information, visit the website for the branch of the military of which your spouse was a member.

13

Division of Debts

Throughout a marriage, most couples will have disagreements about money from time to time. You might think extra money should be spent on a family vacation, and your spouse might insist it should be saved for your retirement. You might think it's time you finally get a new car, and your spouse thinks you would be fine driving the ten-year-old van for two more years.

If you and your spouse had different philosophies about saving and spending during your marriage, chances are you will have some differing opinions when dividing your debts in divorce. What you both can count on is that Florida law provides that, to reach a fair outcome, the payment of debts must also be taken into consideration when dividing the assets from your marriage.

There are steps you can take to ensure the best outcome possible when it comes to dividing your marital debt. These include providing accurate and complete debt information to your lawyer and asking your lawyer to include provisions in your divorce decree to protect you in the future if your spouse refuses to pay his or her share.

Regardless of how the debts from your marriage are divided, know that you will gradually build your independent financial success when making a fresh start after your divorce is final.

13.1   Who is responsible for paying credit card bills and making house payments during the divorce proceedings?

In most cases the court will not make decisions regarding the payment of credit card debt on a temporary basis. Work with your attorney and your spouse to reach a temporary agreement. Discuss the importance of making at least minimum payments on time to avoid substantial finance charges and late fees.

Typically the spouse who remains in the home will be responsible for the mortgage payments, taxes, utilities, and most other ordinary expenses.

If you are concerned that you cannot afford to stay in the marital home on a temporary basis, talk with your attorney about your options prior to your temporary hearing.

13.2   What, if anything, should I be doing with the credit card companies as we go through the divorce?

If possible, it is best to obtain some separate credit prior to the divorce. This will help you establish credit in your own name and help you with necessary purchases following a separation.

Begin by obtaining a copy of your credit report from at least two of the three nationwide consumer reporting companies: Experian, Equifax, or TransUnion. *The Fair Credit Reporting Act* entitles you a free copy of your credit report from each of these three companies every twelve months.

To order your free annual report online, go to www.annualcreditreport.com, call toll-free to (877) 322-8228, or complete an Annual Credit Report Request Form and mail it to: Annual Credit Report Request Service, P.O. Box 105281, Atlanta, Georgia 30348-5281. You can print the form from the Federal Trade Commission website at www.ftc.gov/credit.

Your spouse may have incurred debt using your name. This information is important to relay to your attorney. If you and your spouse have joint credit card accounts, contact any credit card company to close the account. Do the same if your spouse is an authorized user on any of your accounts.

If you want to maintain credit with a company, ask to have a new account in your own name. Be sure to let your spouse know if you close an account he or she has been using.

13.3 How is credit card debt divided?

Credit card debt will be divided as a part of the overall division of the marital property and debts. Just as in the division of property, the court considers what is equitable, or fair, in your case.

If your spouse has exclusively used a credit card for purposes that did not benefit the family, such as gambling, talk with your attorney. In most cases the court will not review a lengthy history of the how you and your spouse used the credit cards but, there can be exceptions.

13.4 Am I responsible for repayment of my spouse's student loans?

It depends. If your spouse incurred student loans prior to the marriage, it is most likely that he or she will be ordered to pay that debt.

If the debt was incurred during the marriage, as a general rule, student loans are considered marital debt. The court can look at the facts of each case to determine the fairness of how the debts will be distributed. The court may also consider payment on student loan debt when calculating the amount of alimony to be paid.

If you were a joint borrower on your spouse's student loan and your spouse fails to pay the loan, the lender may attempt to collect from you even if your spouse has been ordered to pay the debt.

If either you or your spouse has student loan debt, be sure to give your attorney the complete history regarding the debt and ask about the most likely outcome under the facts of your case.

13.5 During the divorce proceedings, am I still responsible for debt my spouse continues to accrue?

It depends. In most cases the court will order each of the parties to be responsible for his or her own post-filing debts.

13.6 During the marriage my spouse applied for and received several credit cards without my knowledge. Am I responsible for them?

It depends. The court will consider the overall fairness of the property and debt division when deciding who should pay this debt. If your spouse bought items with the cards and intends to keep those items, it is likely that she or he will be ordered to pay the debt incurred for the purchases.

The credit card companies are unlikely to be able to pursue collection from you for the debt unless your spouse used them for necessities of life, such as food, necessary clothing, or housing.

13.7 During our marriage, we paid off thousands of dollars of debt incurred by my spouse had before we were married. Will the court take this into consideration when divided our property and debt?

It might. Just as premarital assets can have an impact on the overall division of property and debts, so can premarital debt. Depending upon the length of the marriage, the evidence of the debt, and the amount paid, it may be a factor for the judge to consider.

Be sure to let your attorney know if either you or your spouse brought substantial debt into the marriage.

13.8 Regarding debts, what is a *hold-harmless clause,* and why should it be in the divorce decree?

A *hold-harmless provision* is intended to protect you in the event that your spouse fails to follow a court order to pay a debt after the divorce is granted. The language typically provides that your spouse shall "indemnify and hold (you) harmless from liability" on the debt.

If you and your spouse have a joint debt and your spouse fails to pay, the creditor may nevertheless attempt to collect from you. This is because the court is without power to change the creditor's rights, and can make orders affecting only you and your spouse.

In the event your spouse fails to pay a court-ordered debt and the creditor attempts collection from you, the hold-harmless provision in your divorce decree can be used in an effort to insist that payment is made by your former spouse.

13.9 Why do my former spouse's doctors say they have a legal right to collect from me when my former spouse was ordered to pay her own medical bills?

Your divorce decree does not take away the legal rights of creditors to collect debts. Contact your attorney about your rights to enforce the court order that your spouse pay his or her own medical bills.

13.10 My spouse and I have agreed that I will keep our home; why must I refinance the mortgage?

There may be a number of reasons why your spouse is asking you to refinance the mortgage. First, the mortgage company cannot be forced to take your spouse's name off of the mortgage note. This means that if you did not make the house payments, the lender could pursue collection against your spouse.

Second, your spouse may not want to wait to receive a share of the home equity. It may be possible for you to borrow additional money at the time of refinancing to pay your spouse his or her share of the equity in the home.

Third, the mortgage on your family home may prevent your spouse from buying a home in the future. Because there remains a risk that your spouse could be pursued for the debt to the mortgage company, it is unlikely that a second lender will want to take the risk of extending further credit to your spouse.

13.11 Can I file for bankruptcy while my divorce is pending?

Consult with your attorney if you are considering filing for bankruptcy while your divorce is pending. It will be important for you to ask yourself a number of questions, such as:

- Should I file for bankruptcy on my own or with my spouse?
- How will my filing for bankruptcy affect my ability to purchase a home in the future?
- Which debts can be discharged in bankruptcy, and which cannot?

- How will a bankruptcy affect the division of property and debts in the divorce?
- How might a delay in the divorce proceedings due to a bankruptcy impact my case?
- Which form of bankruptcy is best for my situation?

If you use a different attorney for your bankruptcy than you have for your divorce, be sure that each attorneys is kept fully informed about the developments in the other case.

13.12 What happens if my spouse files for bankruptcy during our divorce?

Contact your attorney right away. The filing of a bankruptcy while your divorce is pending can have a significant impact on your divorce. Your attorney can advise you whether certain debts are likely to be discharged in the bankruptcy, the delay a bankruptcy may cause to your divorce, and whether bankruptcy is an appropriate option for you.

13.13 Can I file divorce while I am in bankruptcy?

Yes, however, you must receive the bankruptcy court's approval with the divorce. While in bankruptcy, your property is protected from debt collection by the "automatic stay." The stay can also prevent the divorce court from dividing property between you and your spouse until you obtain the bankruptcy court's permission to proceed with the divorce.

13.14 What should I do if my former spouse files for bankruptcy after our divorce?

Contact your attorney immediately. If you learn that your former spouse has filed for bankruptcy, you may have certain rights to object to the discharge of any debts your spouse was ordered to pay under your divorce decree. If you fail to take action, it is possible that you will be held responsible for debts your spouse was ordered to pay.

14

Taxes

Nobody likes a surprise letter from the Internal Revenue Service saying he or she owes more taxes. When your divorce is over, you want to be sure that you don't later discover you owe taxes you weren't expecting to pay.

A number of tax issues may arise in your divorce. Your attorney may not be able to answer all of your tax questions, so consulting your accountant or tax advisor for additional advice might be necessary.

Taxes are important considerations in both settlement negotiations and trial preparation. They should not be overlooked. Taxes can impact many of your decisions including those regarding alimony, division of property, and the receipt of benefits.

Be sure to ask the professionals helping you about the tax implications in your divorce so you don't get that letter in the mail that begins, "Dear Taxpayer:…"

14.1 Will either my spouse or I have to pay income tax when we transfer property or pay a property settlement to one another according to our divorce decree?

No. However, it is important that you see the future tax consequences of a subsequent withdrawal, sale, or transfer of certain assets you receive in your divorce.

It is important to ask your attorney to take tax consequences into consideration when looking at the division of your assets.

14.2   Is the amount of child support I pay tax deductible?

No.

14.3   Do I have to pay income tax on any child support I receive?

No. Your child support is tax free regardless of when it is paid or when it is received.

14.4   Is the amount of alimony I am ordered to pay tax deductible?

In many cases, permanent alimony that one spouse pays pursuant to a court order is tax deductible. This will include court-ordered alimony and may also include other forms of support provided to your former spouse, (but not child support). Your tax deduction is a factor to consider when determining a fair amount of alimony to be paid in your case. Some forms of alimony, such as lump sum alimony, may not be tax deductible.

14.5   Do I have to pay tax on the alimony I receive?

In most cases, yes. You must pay income tax on the spousal support you receive. This will include court-ordered alimony and may also include other forms of spousal support, but not child support, paid by your spouse. Some forms of spousal support are not tax deductible and this is a factor that you and your attorney will consider when considering a settlement in your case.

Income tax is a critical factor in determining a fair amount of alimony. Insist that your attorney bring this issue to the attention of your spouse's lawyer, or to the judge, if your case proceeds to trial, so that both the tax you pay and the deduction your spouse receives are taken into consideration.

Be sure to consult with your tax advisor about payment of tax on your spousal support. Making estimated tax payments throughout the year or withholding additional taxes from your wages can avoid a burdensome tax liability at the end of the year.

It is important to budget for payment of tax on your alimony. Taxes are also another item to consider when looking at your monthly living expenses for the purposes of seeking an alimony award.

14.6 During the divorce proceedings, is our tax filing status affected?

It can be. You are considered unmarried if your decree is final by December 31 of the tax year.

If you are considered unmarried, your filing status is either "single" or, under certain circumstances, "head of household." If your decree is not final as of December 31, your filing status is either "married filing a joint return" or "married filing a separate return," unless you live apart from your spouse and meet the exception for "head of household."

While your divorce is in progress, talk to both your tax advisor and your attorney about your filing status. It may be beneficial to figure your tax on both a joint return and a separate return to see which gives you the lower tax. IRS Publication 504, Divorced or Separated Individuals, provides more detail on tax issues while you are going through a divorce.

14.7 Should I file a joint income tax return with my spouse while our divorce is pending?

Consult your tax advisor to determine the risks and benefits of filing of joint return with your spouse. Compare this with the consequences of filing your tax return separately. Often the overall tax liability will be less with the filing of a joint return, but other factors are important to consider.

When deciding whether to file a joint return with your spouse, consider any concerns you have about the accuracy and truthfulness of the information on the tax return. If you have any doubts, consult both your attorney and your tax advisor before agreeing to sign a joint tax return with your spouse. Prior to filing a return with your spouse, try to reach agreement about how any tax owed or refund expected will be shared, and ask your lawyer to assist you in getting this in writing.

14.8 For tax purposes, is one time of year better to divorce than another?

It depends upon your tax situation. If you and your spouse agree that it would be beneficial to file joint tax returns for the year in which you are divorcing, you may wish to not have your divorce finalized before the end of the year.

Your marital status for filing income taxes is determined by your status on December 31. Consequently, if you both want to preserve your right to file a joint return, your decree should not be entered before December 1 of that year.

14.9 What tax consequences should I consider regarding the sale of our home?

When your home is sold, whether during your divorce or after, the sale may be subject to a capital gains tax. If your home was your primary residence and you lived in the home for two of the preceding five years, you may be eligible to exclude up to $250,000 of the gain on the sale of your home. If both you and your spouse meet the ownership and residence tests, you may be eligible to exclude up to $500,000 of the gain.

If you anticipate the gain on the sale of your residence to be over $250,000, talk with your attorney early in the divorce process about a plan to minimize the tax liability. For more information, *see* IRS Publication 523, Selling Your Home, or visit the IRS website at www.irs.gov and talk with your tax advisor.

14.10 How might capital gains tax be a problem for me years after the divorce?

Future capital gains tax on the sale of property should be discussed with your attorney during the negotiation and trial preparation stages of your case. This is especially important if the sale of the property is imminent. Failure to do so may result in an unfair outcome.

For example, suppose you agree that your spouse will be awarded the proceeds from the sale of your home valued at $200,000, after the real estate commission, and you will take the stock portfolio also valued at $200,000.

Suppose that after the divorce, you decide to sell the stock. It is still valued at $200,000, but you learn that its original price was $120,000 and that you must pay capital gains tax of 15 percent on the $80,000 of gain. You pay tax of $12,000, leaving you with $188,000.

Meanwhile, your former spouse sells the marital home but pays no capital gains tax because he qualifies for the $250,000 exemption. He is left with the full $200,000.

Tax implications of your property division should always be discussed with your attorney, with support from your tax advisor as needed.

14.11 During and after the divorce, who gets to claim the children as dependents?

This issue should be addressed in settlement negotiations or at trial, if settlement is not reached.

The judge has discretion to determine which parent will be entitled to claim the children as exemptions for income tax purposes. Where child support has been ordered according to the *Florida Child Support Guidelines,* many judges order that the exemptions be shared or alternated.

If one party has income so low or so high that he or she will not benefit from the dependency exemption, the court may award the exemption to the other parent.

14.12 My decree says I have to sign IRS Form 8332 so my former spouse can claim our child as an exemption, even though I have the substantial amount of parenting time. Should I sign it once for all future years?

No. Parenting time and child support can be modified in the future. If there is a future modification of parenting time or support, which parent is entitled to claim your child as an exemption could change. The best practice is to provide your former spouse a timely copy of Form 8332 signed by you for the appropriate tax year only.

14.13 Can my spouse and I split the child-care tax credit?

According to the *Florida Child Support Guidelines,* the value of the federal income tax credit for child care must be considered when determining the payor spouse's obligation to contribute to child care expenses.

The value of the federal child care tax credit must be subtracted from the actual costs of child care to arrive at a figure for net child-care expenses owed by the spouse paying support.

Only one parent is allowed to claim the credit. If you are the parent paying child care, talk to your lawyer about how to address this issue in your divorce decree.

14.14 Is the cost of getting a divorce, including my attorney fees, tax deductible under any circumstances?

Your legal fees for getting a divorce are not deductible. However, a portion of your attorney fees may be deductible if they are for:

- The collection of sums included in your gross income, such as alimony or interest income
- Advice regarding the determination of taxes or tax due

Attorney fees are "miscellaneous" deductions for individuals and are consequently are limited to 2 percent of your adjusted gross income. More details can be found in IRS Publication 529, Miscellaneous Deductions.

You may also be able to deduct fees you pay to appraisers or accountants who help. Talk to your tax advisor about whether any portion of your attorney fees or other expenses from your divorce is deductible.

14.15 Do I have to complete a new Form W-4 for my employer because of my divorce?

Completing a new Form W-4, Employee's Withholding Certificate, will help you to claim the proper withholding allowances based upon your marital status and exemptions. Also, if you are receiving alimony, you may need to make quarterly estimated tax payments. Consult with your tax advisor to ensure you are making the most preferable tax planning decision.

14.16 What is *innocent spouse relief* and how can it help me?

Innocent spouse relief refers to a method of obtaining relief from the Internal Revenue Service for taxes owed as a result of a joint income tax return filed during your marriage. Numerous factors affect your eligibility for innocent spouse tax relief, such as:

- You would suffer a financial hardship if you were required to pay the tax.

- You did not significantly benefit from the unpaid taxes.
- You suffered abuse during your marriage.
- You thought your spouse would pay the taxes on the original return.

Talk with your attorney or your tax advisor if you are concerned about liability for taxes arising from joint tax returns filed during the marriage. You may benefit from a referral to an attorney who specializes in tax law.

15

Going to Court

For many of us, our images of going to court are created by movie scenes and our favorite television shows. We picture the witness breaking down in tears after a grueling cross examination. We see lawyers waltzing around the courtroom, waving their arms as they plead their case to the jury.

Hollywood drama, however, is a far cry from reality. Going to court for your divorce can mean many things, ranging from sitting in a hallway while waiting for the lawyers and judges to conclude a conference, to being on the witness standing giving mundane answers to questions about your monthly living expenses.

Regardless of the nature of your court proceeding, going to court often evokes a sense of anxiety. Perhaps your divorce might be the first time in your life that you have even been in a courtroom. Be assured that these feelings of nervousness and uncertainty are normal.

Understanding what will occur in court and being well prepared for any court hearings will relieve much of your stress. Knowing the order of events, courtroom etiquette, the role of the people in the courtroom, and what is expected of you will make the entire experience easier.

Your lawyer will be with you at all times to support you any time you go to court. Remember, every court appearance moves you one step closer to completing your divorce so that you can move forward with your life.

15.1 What do I need to know about appearing in court and court dates in general?

Court dates are important. As soon as you receive a notice from your attorney about a court date in your case, confirm whether your attendance will be required and put it on your calendar.

Ask your attorney about the nature of the hearing, including whether the judge will be listening to testimony by witnesses, reading affidavits, or merely listening to the arguments of the lawyers.

Ask whether it is necessary for you to meet with your attorney or take any other action to prepare for the hearing, such as providing additional information or documents.

Find out how long the hearing is expected to last. It may be as short as a few minutes or as long as a day or more.

If you plan to attend the hearing, determine where and when to meet your attorney. Depending upon the type of hearing, your lawyer may want you to arrive in advance of the scheduled hearing time to prepare.

Make sure you know the location of the courthouse, where to park, and the floor and room number of the courtroom. Planning for such simple matters as change for a parking meter can eliminate unnecessary stress. If you want someone to go to court with you to provide you support, check with your attorney first.

15.2 When and how often will I need to go to court?

Whether and how often you will need to go to court depend upon a number of factors. Depending upon the complexity of your case, you may have only one hearing or numerous court hearings throughout the course of your divorce.

Some hearings, usually those on procedural matters, are attended only by the attorneys. These could include requests for the other side to provide information or for the setting of certain deadlines. These hearings are often brief and held in the judge's chambers rather than in the courtroom. Other hearings, such as temporary hearings for custody or support, are typically attended by both parties and their attorneys.

If you and your spouse settle all of the issues in your case, a final hearing will be held. Either, or both of you, depending upon your situation, will be required to attend this brief hearing. If you are the petitioner, the spouse who filed the divorce complaint, plan to attend the final hearing.

If your case proceeds to trial, your appearance will be required for the duration of the trial. In Florida, divorce matters are heard before a judge only; juries do not hear divorces.

15.3 How much notice will I get about appearing in court?

The amount of notice you will get for any court hearing can vary from a few days to several weeks. Ask your attorney whether and when it will be necessary for you to appear in court on your case so that you can have ease in preparing and planning.

If you receive a notice of a hearing, contact your attorney immediately. He or she can tell you whether your appearance is required and what other steps are needed to prepare.

15.4 I am afraid to be alone in the same room with my spouse. When I go to court, is this going to happen if the lawyers go into the judge's office to discuss the case?

Talk to your lawyer. Prior to any court hearing, you and your spouse may be asked to wait while your attorneys meet with the judge to discuss preliminary matters. Some courts have security personnel in the courtroom.

A number of options are likely to be available to ensure that you feel safe. These might include having you or your spouse wait in different locations or having a friend or family member present.

Your lawyer wants to support you in feeling secure throughout all court proceedings. Just let him or her know your concerns.

15.5 Do I have to go to court every time there is a court hearing on any motion?

Not necessarily, however, remember it is your case and you should know what is going on. Discuss this with your attorney. Some matters will be decided by the judge after listening to the arguments of the lawyers.

15.6   My spouse's lawyer keeps asking for *continuances of court dates*. Is there anything I can do to stop this?

Continuances of court dates are not unusual in divorces. A court date might be postponed many reasons. Including a conflict on the calendar of one of the attorneys or the judge, the lack of availability of one of the parties or an important witness, or the need for more time to prepare.

Discuss with your attorney your desire to move your case forward without further delay, so that repeated requests for continuances can be vigorously resisted.

15.7   If I have to go to court, will I be put on the stand? Will there be a jury?

In Florida, divorce matters are heard before a judge only; juries do not hear divorces. Whether you will be put on the stand will depend upon the nature of the issues in dispute, the judge assigned to your case, and your attorney's strategy for your case.

15.8   My lawyer said I need to be in court for our temporary hearing next week. What's going to happen?

A temporary hearing is held to determine such matters as who remains in the house while your divorce is pending, temporary parenting issues, and temporary support.

These hearings can involve testimony from you regarding the children and your financial needs. Most likely you will be asked questions by your attorney and your spouse's attorney will have the opportunity to cross-examine you. You and your attorney should prepare for the possible questions prior to the hearing.

In some counties, your hearing will be one of numerous other hearings. You may find yourself in a courtroom with many other lawyers and their clients, all having matters scheduled before the court that day.

If temporary parenting issues are disputed, you and other witnesses might be required to take the witness stand to give testimony at your temporary hearing. If this is the case, meeting with your attorney in advance to fully prepare is very important.

Talk to your lawyer about the procedure you should expect for the temporary hearing in your case.

15.9 Do I have to go to court if all of the issues in my case are settled?

Generally, a final court hearing will be held even if you and your spouse have settled your case. In most cases only the petitioner, the spouse who filed the divorce complaint, will be required to attend.

If you are the petitioner, plan to attend a final hearing for your divorce. If you are the respondent, the spouse who did not file the complaint, ask your lawyer whether you must attend the final hearing.

In some counties, the court does not require either party to attend and can proceed with "special interrogatories". Check with your attorney for the specific requirements in your county.

15.10 Are there any rules about courtroom etiquette that I need to know?

Every judge will have their own courtroom requirements. Discuss with your attorney whether your judge has specific "does and don'ts." However, keeping in mind a few general tips about being in the courtroom will make your experience easier.

- Dress appropriately.
- Dispose of chewing gum before giving testimony.
- Don't talk aloud in the courtroom unless you're on the witness stand or being questioned by the judge.
- Stand up whenever the judge is entering or leaving the courtroom.
- Be sure to turn off your cell phone and pager.

Although you may feel anxious initially, you'll likely feel more relaxed about the courtroom setting once your hearing gets underway.

15.11 What is the role of the *bailiff?*

The bailiff provides support and security for the judge and lawyers in the management of the court calendar and the courtroom.

15.12 Will there be a *court reporter,* and what will he or she do?

A *court reporter* is a professional trained to make an accurate record of the words spoken and documents offered into evidence during court proceedings. Discuss with your attorney whether a court reporter is necessary for your hearing. A written transcript of a court proceeding may be purchased from the court reporter. If your case is appealed, the transcript prepared by the court reporter will be used by the appeals court to review the facts of your case.

Some hearings are held "off the record," which means that the court reporter is not making a record of what is being said. Ordinarily these are matters for which no appeal is expected to be taken.

15.13 Will I be able to talk to my attorney while we are in court?

During court proceedings it is important that your attorney give his or her attention to anything being said by the judge, witnesses, or your spouse's lawyer. For this reason, your attorney will avoid talking with you when anyone else in the courtroom is speaking.

Plan to have pen and paper with you when you go to court. If your court proceeding is underway and your lawyer is listening to what is being said by others in the courtroom, write him or her a note with your questions or comments.

It is critical that your attorney hear each question asked by the other lawyer and all answers given by each witness. If not, opportunities for making objections to inappropriate evidence may be lost. You can support your attorney in doing an effective job for you by avoiding talking to him or her while a court hearing is in progress.

If your court hearing is lengthy, breaks will be taken. You can use this time to discuss with your attorney any questions or observations you have about the proceeding.

15.14 What questions might my lawyer ask me at the final hearing about the problems in our marriage and why I want the divorce?

Because Florida is a "no-fault" state, your lawyer will ask you questions to show the court that the marriage is irretrievably broken, without going into detail about the specific difficulties in your marriage.

The questions will be similar to these:

Attorney: "Have differences arisen during the course of your marriage?"

Attorney: "Do you believe efforts at reconciliation would be beneficial?"

You: "No."

Attorney: "Is your marriage irretrievable broken?"

You: "Yes."

If your spouse disagrees, he or she may give the opinion that the marriage can be saved. However, most judges recognize that it takes two willing partners for a marriage to be reconciled.

It is unlikely that you will be asked in great detail about the nature of the marital problems that led to the divorce. In the majority of cases, questions like those above will satisfy the judge that the requirements under Florida law for the dissolving of a marriage have been met.

15.15 My lawyer said that the judge has issued a *pretrial order* having to do with my upcoming trial and that we'll have to "comply" with it. What does this mean?

Ask your lawyer for a copy of the pretrial order. Some judges will order that certain information be provided either to the opposing party or to the judge in advance of trial. This might include:

- A list of issues that have been settled
- A list of issues that are still disputed
- Agreements, referred to as *stipulations,* as to the truth of certain facts
- The names of witnesses
- Exhibits
- A summary of how you want the judge to decide the case.

Deadlines are given for providing the information.

15.16 What is a *pretrial conference?*

A *pretrial conference* is a meeting held with the lawyers and the judge to review information related to an upcoming trial, such as how long the trial is expected to last, the issues in dispute, and the law surrounding the disputed issues. Often the trial date is set at the pretrial conference.

If a pretrial conference is held in your case, ask your attorney whether you should attend. Your attorney may request that you either be present for the conference or be available by phone.

15.17 Besides meeting with my lawyer, is there anything else I should do to prepare for my upcoming trial?

Yes. Be sure to review your deposition and any information you provided in your discovery, such as answers to interrogatories. At trial, it is possible that you will be asked some of the same questions. If you think you might give different answers at trial, discuss this with your lawyer.

It is important that your attorney know in advance of trial whether any information you provided during the discovery process has changed.

15.18 I'm meeting with my lawyer to prepare for trial. How do I make the most of these meetings?

Meeting with your lawyer to prepare for your trial is important to achieving a good outcome. Come to the meeting prepared to discuss the following:

- The issues in your case
- Your desired outcome on each of the issues
- The questions you might be asked at trial by both lawyers
- The exhibits that will be offered into evidence during the trial
- The witnesses for your trial
- The status of negotiations

Your meeting with your lawyer will help you better understand what to expect at your trial and make the trial experience easier.

15.19 My lawyer says that the law firm is busy with "trial preparation." What exactly is my lawyer doing to prepare for my trial?

Countless tasks are necessary to perform to prepare your case for trial. These are just some of them:

- Developing arguments to be made on each of the contested issues
- Researching and reviewing the relevant law in your case
- Reviewing the facts of your case to determine which witnesses are best suited to testifying about them
- Reviewing, selecting, and preparing exhibits
- Preparing questions for all witnesses
- Preparing an opening statement
- Reviewing rules on evidence to prepare for any objections to be made or opposed at trial
- Determining the order of witnesses and all exhibits
- Preparing your file for the day of court, including preparing a trial
- Preparing a notebook with essential information

Your lawyer is committed to a good outcome for you in your divorce. He or she will be engaged in many important actions to fully prepare your case for trial.

15.20 My divorce is scheduled for trial. Does this mean there is no hope for a settlement?

Many cases are settled after a trial date is set. The setting of a trial date may cause you and your spouse to think about the risks and costs of going to trial. This can help you and your spouse focus what is most important to you and lead you toward a negotiated settlement. Because the costs of preparing for and proceeding to trial are substantial, it is best to engage in settlement negotiations well in advance of your trial date.

15.21 Can I prevent my spouse from being in the courtroom?

Probably not. Because your spouse has a legal interest in the outcome of your divorce, he or she has a right to be present. Florida courtrooms are open to the public, and it is not uncommon even for persons uninvolved in your divorce to pass through the courtroom at various times simply because they have other business with the court.

15.22 Can I take a friend or family member with me to court?

Yes. Let your attorney know in advance if you intend to bring anyone to court with you. Some people important to you may be very emotional about your divorce or your spouse. Be sure to invite someone who is better able to focus attention on supporting you rather than on his or her own feelings.

15.23 Can my friends and family be present in the courtroom during my trial?

It depends upon whether they will be witnesses in your case. In most cases where witnesses other than the husband and wife are testifying, the attorneys request that the court "sequester" the witnesses. The judge would then order all witnesses, except you and your spouse, to leave the courtroom until after they have testified.

Once a witness has completed his or her testimony, he or she will ordinarily be allowed to remain in the courtroom for the remainder of the trial.

15.24 I want to do a great job testifying as a witness in my divorce trial. What are some tips?

Keep the following in mind to be a good witness on your own behalf:

- Tell the truth. While this may not always be comfortable, it is critical if you want your testimony to be believed by the judge.
- Listen carefully to the complete question before thinking of your answer. Wait to consider your answer until after the full question is asked.
- Slow down. It's easy to speed up our speech when we are anxious. Taking your time with your answers

ensures that the judge hears you and that the court reporter can accurately record your testimony.

- If you don't understand a question or don't know the answer, be sure to say so.
- If the question calls for a "yes" or "no" answer, simply say so. Then wait for the attorney to ask you the next question. If there is more you want to explain, remember that you have already told your attorney, all of the important facts and he or she will make sure you are allowed to give any testimony significant in your case.
- Don't argue with the judge or the lawyers.
- Take your time. You may be asked some questions that call for a thoughtful response. If you need a moment to reflect on an answer before you give it, allow yourself that time.
- Stop speaking if an objection is made by one of the lawyers. Wait until the judge has decided whether to allow you to answer.

15.25 Should I be worried about being cross-examined by my spouse's lawyer at trial?

If your case goes to trial, prepare to be asked some questions by your spouse's lawyer. Many of these questions will call for a simple "yes" or "no."

If you are worried about particular questions, discuss your concerns with your attorney. He or she can support you in giving a truthful response. Focus on preparing well for being asked questions by your spouse's lawyer. Try not take the questions personally; remember that the lawyer is fulfilling a duty to advocate for your spouse's interests. Remember that you are just doing your best to tell the truth about the facts.

15.26 What happens on the day of trial?

Although no two trials are alike, the following steps will occur in most divorce trials:

- The court will ask whether there are any stipulations by the parties—matters that have been agreed to.

- The attorneys will present any motions that need to be addressed by the court before the trial starts.
- Attorneys give opening statements.
- Petitioner's attorney calls petitioner's witnesses to testify. Respondent's attorney may cross-examine each of them.
- Respondent's attorney calls respondent's witnesses to testify. Petitioner's attorney may cross-examine each of them.
- Petitioner's attorney calls any rebuttal witnesses, that is, witnesses whose testimony contradicts the testimony of the respondent's witnesses.
- Closing arguments made first by petitioner's attorney and then by respondent's attorney.

15.27   Will the judge decide my case the day I go to court?

Possibly. Often there is so much information from the trial for the judge to consider that it is not possible for the judge to give an immediate ruling.

The judge may want to review documents, review the law, perform calculations, review his or her notes, and give thoughtful consideration to the issues to be decided. For this reason, it may be days, weeks, or in some cases, even longer before a ruling is made.

When a judge does not make a ruling immediately upon the conclusion of a trial, it is said that the case has been "taken under advisement."

16

The Appeals Process

You may find that despite your best efforts to settle your case, your divorce went to trial and the judge made major decisions that will have a serious impact on your future. You may be either gravely disappointed or even shocked by the judge's ruling.

The judge might have seen your case differently than you and your attorney did. Perhaps the judge made mistakes. Or it may be that Florida law simply does not allow for the outcome you were hoping for.

Whatever the reasons for the court's rulings, you may feel that the judge's decisions are not ones which you can live with. If this is the case, talk to your lawyer immediately about your right to appeal. Together you can decide whether an appeal is in your best interest, or whether it is better to accept the court's ruling and invest your energy in moving forward with your future without an appeal.

16.1 How much time after my divorce do I have to file an appeal?

You must file an appeal within thirty days of the final order you wish to appeal. Because your attorney may also recommend filing certain motions following your trial, discuss your appeal rights with your lawyer as soon as you have received the judge's ruling.

A timely discussion with your attorney about your right to appeal is essential so important deadlines are not missed.

16.2 Can I appeal a temporary order?

Yes, temporary orders can be appealed. Temporary orders that may be appealed include: temporary support, temporary time-sharing, temporary alimony, and temporary exclusive use of the marital home.

16.3 What parts of the decree can be appealed?

If you or your spouse is unhappy with final decisions made by the judge in your case, either of you can file an appeal. Decisions that can be appealed include the parental responsibility, parenting time, child support, alimony, equitable distribution, and attorney's fees.

16.4 Will my attorney recommend I appeal specific aspects of the decree, or will I have to request it?

Your attorney may counsel you to file an appeal on certain issues of your case; you may also ask your lawyer whether there is a legitimate basis for an appeal of any decision you believe is wrong. Talk to your attorney regarding the decisions most dissatisfying to you. Your lawyer can advise which issues have the greatest likelihood of success on appeal, in light of the facts of your case and Florida law.

16.5 When should an appeal be filed?

An appeal should be filed only after careful consultation with your lawyer when you believe that the judge has made a serious error under the law or the facts of your case. Among the factors you and your attorney should discuss are:

- Whether the judge had authority under the law to make the decisions set forth in your decree
- The likelihood of the success of your appeal
- The risk that an appeal by you will encourage an appeal by your former spouse
- The cost of an appeal
- The length of time an appeal can be expected to take
- The impact of a delay in the case during the appeal

The deadline for filing an appeal is thirty days from the date that a final order is entered in your case. It is important that you are clear about the deadline that applies in your case, so talk to your attorney at once if you are thinking about an appeal.

16.6   Are there any disadvantages to filing an appeal?

There can be disadvantages to filing an appeal, including:

- Uncertainty in the outcome
- Increased attorney's fees and costs
- The risk of a worse outcome on appeal than you received at trial
- Delay
- Prolonged conflict between you and your former spouse
- The risk of a second trial occurring after the appeal
- Difficulty in obtaining closure and moving forward with your life

16.7   Is an attorney necessary to appeal?

The appeal process is very detailed and specific, with set deadlines and specific court rules. Given the complex nature of the appellate process, you should have an attorney if you intend to file an appeal.

16.8   How long does the appeals process usually take?

It depends. An appeal can take anywhere from several months to well over a year. An appeal may also result in the appellate court requiring further proceedings by the trial court. This will result in further delay.

16.9   What are the steps in the appeals process?

There are many steps which your lawyer will take on your behalf in the appeal process, including:

- Identifying the issues to be appealed
- Filing a notice with the court of your intent to appeal
- Obtaining the necessary court documents and trial exhibits to send to the appellate court
- Obtaining transcript of trial, a written copy of testimony by witnesses and statements by the judge and the lawyers made in the presence of the court reporter

- Performing legal research to support your arguments on appeal
- Preparing and filing a document known as a "brief," which sets forth the facts of the case and the relevant law, complete with citations to court transcript, court documents, and prior cases
- Possibly making an oral argument before the judges of the appellate court

16.10 Is filing and pursuing an appeal expensive?

Yes. In addition to filing fees and lawyer fees, there is likely to be a substantial cost for the preparation of the transcript of the trial testimony.

16.11 If I do not file an appeal, can I ever go back to court to change my decree?

Certain aspects of a decree are not modifiable, such as the division of property and debts or the award of attorney fees. Other parts of your decree, such as support or matters regarding the children, may be modified if there has been a "material and substantial change in circumstances."

A modification of parental responsibility or parenting time for minor children will also require you to show that the change would be in their best interest.

If your decree did not provide for alimony or if it ordered that the alimony be non-modifiable, it is unlikely that you will have any basis for a modification. If you believe that you have a basis for a modification of your divorce decree, consult with your attorney.

17

What Happens after the Divorce?

You have finally reached the end of your divorce journey. Whether you are feeling sad about the end of your marriage; feeling relieved that it is over and hopeful about your future; or feeling scared about your new life ahead of you, these feeling are normal.

You may also be feeling overwhelmed by the tasks ahead of you. Generally, at this point your attorney will no longer be representing you as you transfer assets or change your name. Make sure you have a game plan and take one step at a time as you move forward with your new life.

17.1 Is there any information I need to give to the court after my divorce?

Generally, the court will have all the information it needs once the *final judgment of dissolution* is entered. When you filed your divorce, your attorney should have provided your social security number, your address, and any other vital information for the court to process the paperwork.

17.2 What if I have moved, should I let the court know?

Yes. Always make sure the court has your current mailing address. This is especially important should your former spouse file any documents in the future or if you are receiving child support or alimony.

17.3 What if I changed employment, should I let the court or anyone else know?

If you are paying any form of support and there is an *income deduction order* directing child support through either the clerk of court or the Florida State Disbursement Center, you will need to let them know so that a new income deduction order can be properly directed to your new employer.

17.4 Do I need to do anything when one of my children is eighteen or nineteen?

No. Florida law requires that the court include provisions for an automatic reduction when you are no longer eligible to receive child support for that child.

17.5 My final judgment includes a provision that my former spouse and I both pay a portion of the children's uninsured medical expenses or other expenses incurred for the minor children. How to I track this information and how and when do I get reimbursed?

Your final judgment should include language on how and when this is to be reimbursed to you. Be sure to keep records and follow the language in your final judgment. Generally, you are required to provide proof of payment to your former spouse and they have a set amount of time in which to send your payment.

Reimbursement of medical expenses and contribution of other expenses is often a matter that arises in post-judgment motions to enforce and contempt. For this reason, it is important to maintain complete records regarding these expenses, such as:

- Copies of all billing statements from the service providers with information regarding your payments, including amount, date, and check number
- Copies of all insurance benefit statements
- Copies of all prescriptions and charges. Your pharmacy can provide you a monthly or annual printout
- If child care is not included in the child support, copies of all checks to the day care providers and a statement directly from the provider of all payments

- Records of all payments for any other court order shared expenses of the children, including sports, music, or other extracurricular activities.

Keep these records as organized as possible in the event there is a future dispute. You may consider a spreadsheet to track expenses and payments. In the event you need to present or defend a case, you will have all the documentation your attorney will need.

17.6 What if my former spouse and I have a disagreement about our parenting plan after the final judgment is entered?

Some final judgments will include a provision that require you to attempt to mediate disputes involving the parenting plan prior to initiating either an enforcement or contempt action. Depending on the dispute, you may want to contact a mediator directly and see if they will mediate the matter without attorneys. If necessary, contact your attorney to discuss your options.

17.7 How do I make payments that were court ordered but are not related to child support or alimony?

Any payments that are not related to support, would be paid directly to the person entitled to the payment. Make sure you keep accurate records of all payments you make in case there is a future dispute.

17.8 My former spouse has not paid me the property settlement as ordered in the final judgment. What can I do?

In the event that your former spouse does not pay court ordered judgments, you may to have to file an enforcement action. If payment becomes an ongoing problem, contact your attorney to discuss your options.

17.9 After my divorce was entered, my former spouse did not pay a judgment and I did not do anything about it. Is it too late?

It depends. Most judgments have a *statute of limitations,* meaning they can only be enforced for a period of time. There are also equitable defenses if too much time has passed since the judgment was entered. If your former spouse is not paying as ordered, you should talk to your attorney and seek a remedy as soon as possible.

17.10 I restored by former name under my divorce decree. What else do I need to do?

The following checklist gives you some guidance of the people and places you may want contact and notify of your new name:

_____Social Security Administration

_____Department of Motor Vehicles (driver's license and vehicle registration)

_____Banking and other financial institutions

_____Insurance (health, life, homeowner's)

_____Creditors (mortgage company, credit card, auto loan companies)

_____Credit reporting agencies

_____Employers

_____Deed and property titles

_____Professional associations/organizations

_____Health care providers, dentist, counselor

_____Post office

_____Public assistance office

_____Schools (yours and your children's)

_____Internal Revenue Service

_____Utility companies (water, electric, trash)

_____Family and friends

_____Accountant

_____Child Support office/Florida State Disbursement Center

_____Department of Vital Statistics

_____Frequent used service providers (hairstylist, lawn care, pool care)

_____Subscriptions, magazines, newspapers

_____Passport services

_____Religious/charitable organizations

_____Registrar of voters

_____Licensing organizations (nursing, bar association, teaching)

_____School alumni organizations

_____Stock certificates

_____Financial planner

17.11 I was told by the driver's license office and others that I need a certified copy of my final judgment of dissolution. How do I get one?

You will need to go directly to the clerk of court of your county and ask for a certified copy. There is usually a fee associated obtaining the certified copy.

17.12 Is there anything else I need to be doing after my final judgment is entered?

We have provided a postdivorce checklist below for you to review and which may be helpful in addressing any actions you may need to take in your particular circumstances.

_____Property

_____Confirm necessary quit claim deeds and real estate transfer documents are filed with the recording office

_____Refinance the mortgage within the time specified in the final judgment

_____File for the homestead exemption with the property appraisers office

_____Complete the exchange of personal property

_____Transfer the title to motor vehicles

_____Transfer or close bank accounts and safe deposit boxes

_____Transfer investment accounts, stocks, and bonds

_____Review beneficiary designations on retirement and financial accounts for any needed changes

_____Insurance

_____Review life insurance beneficiary designations for any needed changes

_____Obtain *COBRA* or other needed health insurance

_____Notify employer to maintain former spouse for six-month period on your health insurance, if applicable

_____Make sure your vehicle is insured in your name

_____If you have minor children, make sure you have insurance cards

_____Debts and liabilities

_____Cancel joint accounts or credit cards, or remove name of former spouse

_____Parenting plan

_____Notify the children's schools if you have sole parental responsibility or ultimate decisions making

_____Child support and alimony

_____If ordered to receive child support, make sure your address is current with the clerk of court or the Florida State Disbursement Unit

_____If you are ordered to pay child support, make sure your employer information is current with the clerk of court and the Florida State Disbursement Unit

_____If you are ordered to pay alimony only, generally the payment is make directly to your former spouse. If order to pay through the clerk of court, make sure your contact information and employer information is current

_____Uninsured medical expenses

_____Make sure you keep good records of all payments.

_____If ordered to submit the invoices to your former spouse within a specified time period, make sure you mail them in a timely manner

_____If you are ordered to reimburse your former spouse for the uninsured medical expenses make sure you send payment in a timely manner

_____Tax matters

_____Notify your employer in your change of exemption status (complete a new W-4)

_____In necessary, notify the IRS on Form 8822 for a change in address

_____Refer to IRS Publication 504 for more information related to being "Divorced or Separated"

_____Attorney's fees

_____Make arrangement with your attorney to pay any outstanding attorney's fees

_____If your former spouse was ordered to pay all or a portion of your attorney's fees, discuss options with your attorney if they remain unpaid

_____If you are ordered to pay all or a portion of your former spouse's attorney's fees make arrangements for payment

_____Name change–*See* previous chart

_____Estate Planning

_____Review your will and powers of attorney to determine if you need to make changes

_____If changes are necessary, make an appointment with your attorney to make the changes to your will or create a will, powers of attorney, living will and other important estate planning documents

In Closing

In the months ahead, your divorce will come to an end. Acknowledge yourself for the courage and strength you have shown during the process. You have made difficult decisions that affect you, your children's needs, and your life goals. Now you have the opportunity for a new future. You have the opportunity to focus on you and your children, your living situation, your financial security, and your personal growth and healing. You can take action to propel yourself into a world of new possibilities.

It is time to take inventory of the lessons learned, goals met, and actions yet to be taken. Celebrate each step forward and be kind to yourself over the occasional missteps backwards. You have transitioned through what can be one of hardest times in your life. All the best to you in your new life ahead.

Resources

Florida Clerk of Courts
(850) 922-5081
www.flcourts.org
The Florida Courts website provides a court locator for you to find your local clerk's offices as well as self-help forms, a list of all Legal Aid services throughout the state, self-help centers in your area, and Florida Family Law Rules and opinions

Florida Department of Revenue
Child Support Customer Service
(800) 622-KIDS (5437)
www.dor.myflorida.com
The Florida Department of Revenue website will direct you to your nearest child support office, allow you to apply for services online, and check the status of payments.

Florida Coalition Against Domestic Violence
(800) 500-1119
www.facdv.org
Please contact for a certified shelter in your area

National Domestic Violence Hotline
(800)799-7233
www.thehotline.org

Department of Children and Families
Abuse Hotline
(800) 962-2873

Social Security Administration (SSA)
(800) 772-1213
www.ssa.org
Website allows users to apply for various services, get replacement cards, change address and get additional information

Annual Credit Report Request Services
(877) 322-8228
www.annualcreditreport.com
Website allows you to request an annual credit report

Internal Revenue Service (IRS)
(800) 829-1040 for personal tax questions
www.irs.com
The website offers IRS publications and forms available for download

The Florida Bar
651 E. Jefferson Street
Tallahassee, FL 32399-2300
(800) 342-8011
(850) 561-5844
www.floridabar.org
On the Florida Bar website you are able to search for a lawyer or get a referral for a lawyer in your community. If your community has a local bar that provides referrals, the Florida Bar website will direct you to your local bar association.

Glossary

Affidavit: A written statement of facts made under oath and signed before a notary public. Affidavits are used primarily when there will not be a hearing in open court with live testimony. The attorney will prepare an affidavit to present relevant facts. Affidavits may be signed by the parties or in some cases by witnesses. The person signing the affidavit may be referred to as the *affiant*.

Allegation: A statement that one party claims is true.

Alimony: Court-ordered spousal support payments from one party to another, often to enable the recipient spouse to become economically independent.

Answer: A written response to the petition for divorce. It serves to admit or deny the allegations in the complaint and may also make claims against the opposing party. This is sometimes called a *responsive pleading*. An answer should be filed within twenty days of either (a) the complaint being served by the sheriff or (b) the respondent's voluntary acceptance of service being filed with the court.

Appeal: The process by which a higher court reviews the decision of a lower court. In Florida family law cases, a person will first file an appeal with the Florida Court of Appeals. After that appeal is decided there may be a further appeal to the Florida Supreme Court.

Child support: Financial support for a child paid by the noncustodial parent to the custodial parent.

Court order acceptable for processing (COAP): A type of court order that provides for payment of civil service retirement to a former spouse.

183

Contempt of court: The willful and intentional failure of a party to comply with a court order, judgment, or decree. Contempt may be punishable by a fine or jail.

Contested case: Any case in which the parties cannot reach an agreement. A contested case will result in a trial to have the judge decide disputed issues.

Court order: A court-issued document setting forth the judge's orders. An order can be issued based upon the parties' agreement or the judge's decision. An order may require the parties to perform certain acts or set forth their rights and responsibilities. An order is put in writing, signed by the judge, and filed with the court.

Cross-examination: The questioning of a witness by the opposing counsel during trial or at a deposition, in response to questions asked by the other lawyer.

Deposition: A witness's testimony taken out of court, under oath, and in the presence of lawyers and a court reporter. If a person gives a different testimony at the time of trial, he or she can be impeached with the deposition testimony; that is, statements made at a deposition can be used to show untruthfulness if a different answer is given at trial.

Direct examination: The initial questioning of a witness in court by the lawyer who called him or her to the stand.

Discovery: A process used by attorneys to discover information from the opposing party for the purpose of fully assessing a case for settlement or trial. Types of discovery include interrogatories, requests for production of documents, and requests for admissions.

Dissolution: The act of terminating or dissolving a marriage.

Equitable distribution of property: The method by which real and personal property and debts are divided in a divorce. Given all economic circumstances of the parties, Florida law requires that marital property and debts be divided in a equitable manner.

Final judgment of dissolution: A final court order dissolving the marriage, dividing property and debts, ordering support, and entering other orders regarding finances and the minor children.

Glossary

Ex parte orders: Usually in reference to a motion, the term used to describe an appearance of only one party before the judge, without other party being present. For example, an *ex parte* restraining order may be granted immediately after the filing of petition for injunction for protection against domestic violence.

Guardian *ad litem* (GAL): A person, often a lawyer or mental health professional, appointed by court to conduct an investigation regarding the children's best interest.

Hearing: Any proceeding before the court for the purpose of resolving disputed issues between the parties through presentation of testimony, affidavits, exhibits, or argument.

Hold-harmless clause: A term in a court order that requires one party to assume responsibility for a debt and to protect the other spouse from any loss or expense in connection with it, as in "to hold harmless from liability."

Interrogatories: Written questions sent from one party to the other that are used to obtain facts or opinions related to the divorce.

Irreconcilable differences: The standard necessary for the court to grant a divorce in Florida. These are differences in the marriage that make it impossible to the marriage to be restored.

Mediation: A process by which a neutral third party facilitates negotiations between the parties on a wide range of issues.

Mediation agreement: A written agreement of the terms agreed to in mediation. The mediation agreement can be a partial agreement where only some issues have been agreed to or a full agreement where all issues of the divorce have been agreed to.

Motion: A written application to the court for relief, such as temporary child support, custody, or restraining orders.

No-fault divorce: The type of divorce Florida has that court does not require evidence of marital misconduct. This means that abandonment, cruelty, and adultery are neither relevant nor required to be proven for the purposes of granting the divorce.

Notice of hearing: A written statement sent to the opposing lawyer or spouse listing the date and place of a hearing and the nature of the matters that will be heard by the court. In Florida, one party is required to give the other party reasonable notice of any court hearing.

Parenting plan: Written agreement or court order that details parental responsibilities and time sharing agreements.

Party: The person in a legal action whose rights or interests will be affected by the divorce. For example, in a divorce the parties include the wife and husband.

Pending: During the case. For example, the judge may award you temporary support while your case is pending.

Petition for dissolution of marriage: The first document filed with the clerk of the court in an action for divorce, separation, or paternity. The petition sets forth the facts on which the requested relief is based.

Petition for relocation: A parent's written request to the court seeking permission to relocate to another state with the children.

Petitioner: A term used to refer to the person who files the petition seeking a divorce.

Pleadings: Documents filed with the court seeking a court order.

Post-Judgment: Any court filings that occur after the final judgment of dissolution is entered.

Qualified domestic relations order (QDRO): A type of court order that provides for direct payment from a retirement account to a former spouse.

Qualified medical support order (QMSO): A type of court order that provides a former spouse certain rights regarding medical insurance and information.

Request for production of documents: A written request for documents sent from one party to the other during the discovery process.

Respondent: The responding party to a divorce; the party who did not file the petition initiating the divorce.

Sequester: To order prospective witnesses out of the courtroom until they have concluded giving their testimony.

Set off: A debt or financial obligation of one spouse that is deducted from the debt or financial obligation of the other spouse.

Settlement: The agreed resolution of disputed issues.

Shared parental responsibility: The legal right and responsibility awarded by a court for the decision making for a minor child.

Show cause: Written application to the court to hold another person in contempt of court for violating or failing to comply with a current court order.

Sole parental responsibility: The legal right and responsibility awarded by the court to one parent to make decisions affecting the minor child.

Sole parental responsibility with ultimate decision making: The legal right and responsibility awarded by the court to one parent to make decisions affecting the minor child after talking with the other parent.

Stipulation: An agreement reached between parties or an agreement by their attorneys.

Subpoena: A document delivered to a person or witness that requires him or her to appear in court, appear for a deposition, or produce documents. Failure to comply could result in punishment by the court. A subpoena requesting documents is called a *subpoena duces tecum.*

Supplemental petition to modify: A party's written request to the court to change a prior order regarding custody, child support, alimony or any other order that the court may change by law.

Temporary restraining order: An order of the court prohibiting a party from certain behavior. For example, a temporary restraining order may order a person not to transfer any funds during a pending divorce action.

Trial: A formal court hearing in which the judge will decide disputed issues raised by the parties' pleadings.

Under advisement: A term used to describe the status of a case, usually after a court hearing on a motion or a trial, when the judge has not yet made a decision.

Index

Index

191

About the Authors

Lisa P. Kirby, Esq., is a family law attorney in private practice in Naples, Florida.

A native of Florida, she lived in various states across the United States and in Ninomiya, Japan, before returning to Florida to practice law in Naples.

She earned a bachelor of arts degree in English from Arizona State University in Tempe, Arizona, before she attended Cleveland-Marshall College of Law, in Cleveland, Ohio. Ms. Kirby returned to Florida to work as an assistant public defender in Collier County, Florida. In January 2000, she began her family law practice and has enjoyed helping couples and families navigate the court system.

Ms. Kirby has worked with the Shelter for Abused Women and Children and has spoken at training seminars on the legal aspects of domestic violence issues. Her philosophy in working with clients involves empowering them so that they understand the court system and can be the realistic about results to expect in their cases. Ms. Kirby may be reached through her website at: **www.ckcattorneys.com.**

Shayna K. Cavanaugh, Esq., practices law in Naples, Florida, where she is the owner of the Law Office of Shayna K. Cavanaugh, P.A. She began practicing law in 1996 in Oklahoma City, Oklahoma, where she earned her law degree from Oklahoma City University School of Law. Prior to attending law school, she received her bachelor of arts degree in journalism and public relations from Arizona State University in Tempe, Arizona. She moved to Naples in 1997 and started her career practicing family law, which has included divorce, domestic violence cases, and guardianship. Prior to starting her own practice, Ms. Cavanaugh was an attorney for legal aid, working with clients who had limited means and high needs in their divorces.

Throughout her career she has handled hundreds of divorce cases, including complex matters involving domestic violence, parenting issues, relocation issues, and support issues. She has also helped hundreds of clients achieve a negotiated agreement through mediation by focusing on a client-centered approach.

Ms. Cavanaugh is passionate about helping clients, and her focus on what is most important to them. She strives to give her clients the support, advice, and guidance they need throughout the divorce process.

Ms. Cavanaugh has spoken on the topic of domestic violence and divorce while collaborating with the Shelter for Abused Women and Children, serving as their contract attorney from 2003-2009. She has served on panels with judges, advocates, and psychologists to engage in discussions about how domestic violence impacts the spouses and children of divorce. Ms. Cavanaugh has been a guest instructor at local colleges and universities on the issues of Family Law and Domestic Violence. She was involved in the Collier County Coalition Against Domestic Violence, in which she coordinated with the local shelter, Children's Advocacy Center, Law Enforcement, and various other organization throughout Collier County, to create resources for victims of domestic violence.

Ms. Cavanaugh was also the recipient of the "Giving Back" award from Legal Aid of Collier County. In 2016, she received recognition as a "Top 10" in client satisfaction by the American Institute of Family Law Attorneys. She is a member of the Florida Bar Association and Collier County and Women's Bar Associations. She may be reached through her website at **www.cavanaughfamilylaw.com.**

Divorce Titles from Addicus Books

Visit our online catalog at www.AddicusBooks.com

Divorce in Alabama: The Legal Process, Your Rights, and What to Expect $21.95

Divorce in Arizona: The Legal Process, Your Rights, and What to Expect. $21.95

Divorce in California: The Legal Process, Your Rights, and What to Expect $21.95

Divorce in Connecticut: The Legal Process, Your Rights, and What to Expect $21.95

Divorce in Florida: The Legal Process, Your Rights, and What to Expect $21.95

Divorce in Georgia: Simple Answers to Your Legal Questions $21.95

Divorce in Hawaii: The Legal Process, Your Rights, and What to Expect $21.95

Divorce in Illinois: The Legal Process, Your Rights, and What to Expect $21.95

Divorce in Louisiana: The Legal Process, Your Rights, and What to Expect $21.95

Divorce in Maine: The Legal Process, Your Rights, and What to Expect $21.95

Divorce in Michigan: The Legal Process, Your Rights, and What to Expect. $21.95

Divorce in Mississippi: The Legal Process, Your Rights, and What to Expect. $21.95

Divorce in Missouri: The Legal Process, Your Rights, and What to Expect $21.95

Divorce in Nebraska: The Legal Process, Your Rights, and What to Expect—2nd Edition $21.95

Divorce in Nevada: The Legal Process, Your Rights, and What to Expect. $21.95

Divorce in New Jersey: The Legal Process, Your Rights, and What to Expect $21.95

Divorce in New York: The Legal Process, Your Rights, and What to Expect $21.95

Divorce in North Carolina: The Legal Process, Your Rights, and What to Expect $21.95

Divorce in Tennessee: The Legal Process, Your Rights, and What to Expect $21.95

Divorce in Virginia: The Legal Process, Your Rights, and What to Expect $21.95

Divorce in Washington: The Legal Process, Your Rights, and What to Expect $21.95

Divorce in West Virginia: The Legal Process, Your Rights, and What to Expect $21.95

Divorce in Wisconsin: The Legal Process, Your Rights, and What to Expect $21.95

To Order Books:
Visit us online at: www.AddicusBooks.com
Call toll free: (800) 888-4741

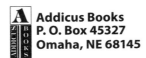

Addicus Books
P. O. Box 45327
Omaha, NE 68145

To order books from Addicus Books:

Please send:

_____copies of_____
                                        (Title of book)
        at $ _____each   TOTAL   _____
        NE residents add 5% sales tax   _____

        Shipping/Handling
            $6.75 for first book
            $1.10 for each additional book _____

                TOTAL ENCLOSED   _____

Name _____
Address _____
City _____State_____Zip _____

☐ Visa   ☐ Mastercard   ☐ AMEX   ☐ Discover
Credit card number _____
Expiration date _____
Four digit CVV number on back of card _____

Order by credit card or personal check.

To Order Books:
Visit us online at: www.AddicusBooks.com
Call toll free: (800) 888-4741

Addicus Books
P. O. Box 45327
Omaha, NE 68145